The COMPANIONS in Christ Network

www.companionsinchrist.org

So much more!

Companions in Christ offers leaders *so much more* than just printed resources. It offers an ongoing LEADERSHIP NETWORK that provides:

- Opportunities to connect with other churches who are also journeying through *Companions in Christ*
- Helpful leadership tips and articles as well as updated lists of supplemental resources
- Training opportunities that develop and deepen the leadership skills used in formational groups
- A staff available to consult with you to meet the needs of your small group
- An online discussion room where you can share or gather information
- Insights and testimonies from other *Companions in Christ* leaders
- A FREE 48-page *Getting Started Guide* filled with practical tools to help you start a group in your church
- FREE *Companions in Christ* posters to use as you promote the group in your congregation

Just complete this card and drop it in the mail, and you can enjoy the many benefits available to leaders through the *Companions in Christ* NETWORK!

❏ Add my name to the *Companions in Christ* NETWORK <u>mailing list</u> so that I can receive ongoing information about small-group resources and leadership trainings.

❏ Add my name to the *Companions in Christ* NETWORK <u>email list</u> so that I can receive ongoing information about small-group resources and leadership trainings.

❏ Please send me a FREE 48-page *Getting Started Guide.*

❏ Please send me FREE *Companions in Christ* posters. Indicate quantity needed: _____

Name: _____

Address: _____

City/State/Zip: _____

Church: _____

Email: _____ Phone: _____

D1298507

WOBLG

Fold here and tape.

For information about *Companions in Christ* visit

www.companionsinchrist.org

Please include your return address:

_____

_____

_____

||||

BUSINESS REPLY MAIL
FIRST-CLASS MAIL PERMIT NO. 1540 NASHVILLE TN

POSTAGE WILL BE PAID BY ADDRESSEE

COMPANIONS *in Christ*

UPPER ROOM MINISTRIES
PO BOX 340012
NASHVILLE TN 37203-9540

I..II I..I..I..I.I III....II.I.I..I.I..I.I.IIII..I..II

COMPANIONS

in Christ

The Way of
Blessedness

LEADER'S GUIDE

Stephen D. Bryant

UPPER
ROOM BOOKS
NASHVILLE

COMPANIONS IN CHRIST: THE WAY OF BLESSEDNESS
Leader's Guide
Copyright © 2003 by Upper Room Books®
All rights reserved.

The Upper Room® Web site http://www.upperroom.org

Cover design: Bruce Gore
Design and implementation: Lori Putnam
Cover art: Carter Bock
Cover art rendering: Marjorie J.Thompson
First printing: 2003

Library of Congress Cataloging-in-Publication

Bryant, Stephen D.
Companions in Christ: the way of blessedness: leader's guide /
Stephen D. Bryant
      p. cm.
   Includes bibliographical references.
   ISBN 0-8358-0994-3
   1. Christian life—Biblical teaching. 2. Beatitudes—Study and teaching. 3. Small groups—Religious aspects—Christianity—Study and teaching. I. Thompson, Marjorie J., 1953– Companions in Christ: the way of blessedness. II. Title.
BV4501.3.B79 2003
226.9'306—dc21   2003010101

For more information on *Companions in Christ*
call 1-800-972-0433 or visit www.companionsinchrist.org

Contents

Weekly Needs at a Glance

*P*rior to your first *Way of Blessedness* meeting, review this Weekly Needs at a Glance list to familiarize yourself with items needed at the Preparatory Meeting. This is also a good time to review what is needed at each of the weekly meetings. Knowing well in advance the items required for each meeting will help you avoid last-minute crises. All items but one are familiar and readily available. The "oil button" is an item that may be unfamiliar. This is a small one-inch-diameter container of solid oil available through most Christian bookstores. If you prefer, you may substitute any fragrant oil placed in a small container with a secure lid.

Weekly Materials

ALL MEETINGS

- Christ candle (large white pillar candle) or other central candle (such as the Companions Circle of Friends Candleholder) and cloth for worship table
- Hymnals, songbooks, or other arrangements for music (tapes/CDs and player)
- Extra Bibles
- Group ground rules developed during your Preparatory Meeting, printed on newsprint and posted in your meeting room
- "Candle Prayer," printed on newsprint and posted in your meeting room (if you choose to use this prayer as a group):

Light of Christ
Shine on our path
Chase away all darkness
and lead us to the heart of God.
Amen.

- Optional: Newsprint and markers; chalkboard or whiteboard
- Optional: Symbol on worship table for link with a partner group (consider a smaller candle or perhaps a postcard or gift from the partner group)

PREPARATORY MEETING

- Participant's Book for each member
- Printout from the Web site www.companionsinchrist.org (*The Way of Blessedness* groups area)
- "Prayer for Our Companions in Christ Groups" card found in the back of this Leader's Guide
- Optional: A copy of the "Holy Listening Exercise" and "Review Questions" (pages 30–31) for each participant

WEEK 1   EXPLORING THE BLESSED LIFE

- Scripture references (page 33) on newsprint to post in room
- Printed blessings (two) from the "Closing" (pages 37–38) on newsprint or board
- Note: A copy of "Sharing Spiritual Journeys, Questions for Daily Reflection and Journaling" (page 40) for each participant (for use with the elective optional week)

OPTIONAL WEEK   SHARING SPIRITUAL JOURNEYS

- Extra copies of "Sharing Spiritual Journeys, Questions for Daily Reflection and Journaling" (page 40) if needed by participants

WEEK 2   EMBRACING OUR SPIRITUAL POVERTY

- A copy of the "Closed Hands, Open Hands" (page 45) meditation for each participant

WEEK 3   TEARS AS ANGUISH, TEARS AS GIFT

- A copy of "Lamenting Our Loss on the Emmaus Road" (page 52) for each group member

- Art supplies such as construction paper, glue, scissors, colored pencils, play dough or clay
- A bell or chime
- Room set up as described in "Prepare materials and the meeting space"
- Two pieces of pita bread broken in pieces and placed in a basket
- Small cruet of fragrant oil or an oil button

WEEK 4   THE POWER OF A CLEAR AND GENTLE HEART
- No arrangements beyond those listed under "All Meetings"

WEEK 5   A SATISFYING HUNGER AND THIRST
- A copy of "Developing a Rule of Life" (page 65) and "Rule of Life Notes" (page 66) for each group member
- Pencils, crayons, and paper

WEEK 6   EMBRACING THE WISDOM OF TENDERNESS
- A copy of the "Jonah Story Reflection Sheet" (page 71) for each participant
- Pictures cut from newspapers or magazines depicting people in painful or difficult circumstances (persons with AIDS, people living in extreme poverty, war refugees, etc.)
- Newsprint and markers

WEEK 7   RECEIVING THE VISION OF GOD
- Special room arrangement as described in "Prepare materials and the meeting space"
- A copy of "Beholding the Blessing in One Another" (page 76) for each participant

WEEK 8   MAKING PEACE, AN OFFERING OF LOVE
- Enough copies of "Scenarios for Practicing Peace" (pages 81–82) to provide each member with one scenario
- A copy of "A Path to Becoming Peacemakers" (pages 83–84) for each participant
- Selection, based on the Leader's Notes titled "Selecting a Peacemaking Issue" (page 85), of a generally known divisive issue that engages everyone

WEEK 9   THE DEEP GLADNESS OF SUFFERING LOVE

- Reminders to group members early in the week about bringing an object representative of their rule of life
- A copy of "A Covenant Prayer in the Wesleyan Tradition" sheet (page 92) and the "Closing Litany" (pages 93–94) for each participant
- Optional: A card or other form of communication to send to your partner group

Acknowledgments

The original twenty-eight-week *Companions in Christ* resource grew from the seeds of a vision long held by Stephen D. Bryant, editor and publisher of Upper Room Ministries, and given shape by Marjorie J. Thompson, director of the Pathways Center of Upper Room Ministries and spiritual director to the *Companions in Christ* Network. The vision, which has now expanded into the Companions in Christ series, was realized through the efforts of many people over many years. The original advisors, consultants, authors, editors, and test churches are acknowledged in the foundational twenty-eight-week resource, as well as in the second title of the series, *Companions in Christ: The Way of Forgiveness*. We continue to owe an immense debt of gratitude to each person and congregation named.

Companions in Christ: The Way of Blessedness is the third title in a series of shorter small-group resources that build on the foundation of *Companions in Christ*. The progression for the nine-week journey of *The Way of Blessedness* and the writing of the weekly articles in the Participant's Book are the primary work of Marjorie Thompson. The daily exercises in the Participant's Book and the deeper explorations in the Leader's Guide are the primary work of Stephen Bryant. A staff advisory team comprised of Lynne Deming, Cindy Helms, Tony Peterson, and Marjorie Thompson contributed to the completion of the Leader's Guide. Mary Lou Redding served as a consultant and contributor of several ideas that influenced the final content of the Participant's Book. In addition, several Companions trainers offered valuable insight and guidance for developing *The Way of Blessedness*. This group included John Anderson, Ron Lagerstrom, Larry Peacock, Deborah Suess, Wynn McGregor, and Carole Cotton Winn.

Introduction

Welcome to *Companions in Christ: The Way of Blessedness*, a small-group resource designed to help your small group explore and experience more deeply the blessed life Jesus describes in the Beatitudes. These challenging teachings from the Sermon on the Mount provide a window through which your group members can glimpse the kingdom of God, a view revealed through the eyes and words of Christ.

The Beatitudes furnish the key to realizing God's joy-filled intent for Christian disciples, to living the soul-deep gladness and satisfaction of our faith. The path to which Christ calls us is not easy. Initially his teachings may strike us as strange or confusing. It requires strong commitment to understand and practice these truths. As you move onward with your group, we trust you will discover together the joy of the way of blessedness.

In response to small groups who want to continue their exploration of spiritual practices that began with the original twenty-eight-week *Companions in Christ* resource, The Upper Room is developing the Companions in Christ series. *The Way of Forgiveness*, the second title in the series, offers a journey through the forgiven and forgiving life, keeping God's grace always before our eyes. *The Way of Blessedness* is the third title in the series.

Each resource in the Companions series expands the foundational content of the twenty-eight-week resource and uses the same basic format. The foundational resource, *Companions in Christ*, explored the Christian spiritual life under five headings: Journey, Scripture, Prayer, Call, and Spiritual Guidance. Each supplementary volume of the Companions in Christ series will explore in greater depth some aspect of one of these primary categories of spiritual practice.

The Way of Blessedness falls under the general heading of Scripture. The eight Beatitudes, found in Matthew 5:3-10, open Jesus' Sermon on the Mount (Matthew 5–7). Each statement is concise and direct, yet layered with profound wisdom. To explore the depth of these words, we will engage the Bible with mind and heart by drawing on classic practices of scriptural meditation and prayer. Keep in mind that this resource is not a Bible study in any traditional sense. It represents a formational approach to scripture more than an informational approach. Our interest lies in exploring the Beatitudes as a pathway of spiritual formation, discovering how the blessed life helps shape us into the fullness of the image of Christ.

About the Resource and Process

Like all resources in the Companions in Christ series, *The Way of Blessedness* has two primary components: (1) individual reading and daily exercises throughout the week with the Participant's Book and (2) a weekly two-hour meeting based on directions in the Leader's Guide. The Participant's Book has a weekly reading that introduces new material and five daily exercises to help participants reflect on their lives in light of the reading's content. These exercises help participants move from information (knowledge about) to experience (knowledge of). An important part of this process is keeping a personal notebook or journal; participants record reflections, prayers, and questions for later review and for reference at the weekly group meeting. The daily exercise commitment is about thirty minutes. The weekly meeting includes time for reflecting on the past week's exercises, for moving deeper into learnings from the weekly readings, and for engaging in group experiences of worship.

The material in *Companions in Christ: The Way of Blessedness* covers a period of ten weeks, a preparatory meeting followed by nine weeks of content that moves through each of the following areas:

1. *Exploring the Blessed Life*: Introduction to the blessed life in relation to God's reign

2. *Embracing Our Spiritual Poverty*: Learning to cherish our dependence on God's grace

3. *Tears As Anguish, Tears As Gift*: Uncovering the blessings hidden in mourning our losses

4. *The Power of a Clear and Gentle Heart*: Recovering the meaning and strength of meekness

5. *A Satisfying Hunger and Thirst*: Claiming the satisfactions of yearning for God's reign

6. *Embracing the Wisdom of Tenderness*: Opening our small hearts to God's great heart of mercy

7. *Receiving the Vision of God*: Learning to see God and to see as God sees

8. *Making Peace, an Offering of Love*: Receiving God's peace so we may share it

9. *The Deep Gladness of Suffering Love*: Finding the joy in suffering for Christ's sake

Option to Add Week on Sharing Spiritual Journeys

The opportunity for group members to share their spiritual journeys has been identified as one of the most effective ways for groups to form a genuine sense of community and mutual commitment. This sharing is an important component of Part 1 in the twenty-eight-week foundational *Companions in Christ* resource. Therefore the option of an additional week is included in this Leader's Guide for *The Way of Blessedness*. After Week 1, you may, with group consent, add a week to give members the chance to share something of their spiritual journeys with one another. This optional session will be especially helpful if your group members are not well acquainted or if your group has not yet experienced the twenty-eight-week original *Companions* program. Even if your group has shared personal journeys before, individuals will have grown in certain ways since then. Participants may discover new movements of God's grace in their lives through this sharing.

If you believe your group members would benefit from such a week, tell them of the opportunity at the Preparatory Meeting and ask them to consider it. Then before the "Closing" for Week 1, seek the consensus of the group. If the members agree to the additional week, hand out the sheet titled "Sharing Spiritual Journeys, Questions for Daily Reflection and Journaling." The sheet contains six questions, one for each day before the group meeting. Based on the number in your group, calculate the amount of time each person may have for sharing and communicate this amount of time clearly to the participants. They will not be able to tell their life stories, but rather thoughtfully focused aspects of their spiritual journeys. Remember that you will join the group in this sharing process.

The Companions in Christ Network

An added dimension of *Companions in Christ: The Way of Blessedness* is the Network. While you and your group are experiencing *The Way of Blessedness*, groups in other congregations will also be meeting. The Network provides opportunities for you to share your experiences with one another and to link in a variety of meaningful ways. In the Preparatory Meeting you will be invited to pray for another group, send greetings or encouragement, or receive their support for your group. Connecting in these ways will enrich your group's experience and the experience of those to whom you reach out.

The Network also provides a place for sharing conversation and information. The *Companions* Web site, www.companionsinchrist.org, includes a discussion room where you can offer insights, voice questions, and respond to others in an ongoing process of shared learning. The site provides a list of other *Way of Blessedness* groups and their geographical locations so you can make contact as you feel led. Locations and dates for Leader Orientation training events (basic one-day trainings) and the Leader Trainings events (advanced three-day trainings) are posted here.

The Role of the Small-Group Leader

Leading a group for spiritual formation differs in many ways from teaching a class. The most obvious difference is in your basic goal as group leader. In a class, you have specific information (facts, theories, ways of doing things) that you want to convey. You can gauge your success at the end of the class by participants' grasp of the information. In a group for spiritual formation, your goal is to enable spiritual growth in each group member. You work in partnership with the Holy Spirit, who alone can bring about transformation of the human heart. Here gaining wisdom is more important than gaining knowledge, and growing in holiness is more important than gaining either knowledge or wisdom. Success, if it has any meaning in this context, will be evident over months and even years in the changed lives of group members.

Classes tend to be task-oriented. Groups for spiritual formation tend to be more process-oriented. Even though group members will have done common preparation in reading and daily exercises, group discussions may move in directions you do not expect. You will need to be open to the Holy Spirit's movement and vigilant in discerning the difference between following the Spirit's lead and going off on a tangent. Such discernment requires careful, prayerful listening—a far more important skill in your role as group leader than talking.

Finally, classes have as their primary focus some set of objective data: a Bible passage, information from a book, or interpretations of current events. A group for spiritual formation, however, focuses on the personal faith experience of each group member. Each person seeks to understand and be open to the grace and revelation of God. Even when group members have read and reflected on a scripture passage, the basis for group discussion is not "What did the author intend to say to readers of that time?" but "How does this passage connect to my life or illuminate my experience?" Discussion will be a sharing of experience, not a debate over ideas. You will model this type of personal sharing with your group because of your involvement in all parts of the group meeting. The type of leadership needed differs from that of a traditional teacher of a church school class or small-group facilitator. As leader, you will read the material and complete the daily exercises along with other members and bring your responses to share with the group. You lead by offering your honest reflections and by trying to enable the group members to listen carefully to one another and to the Spirit in your midst.

Leading a group for spiritual formation requires particular qualities. Foremost among these are patience and trust. You will need patience to allow the sessions to unfold as they will. Spiritual formation is a lifelong process. Identifying any great leaps forward during the several weeks the group will spend on *The Way of Blessedness* may be difficult. It may even take a while for group members to adjust to the purpose and style of a formational group process. As a group leader, resolve to ask questions with no "right" answers in mind and to encourage participants to talk about their own experience. Setting an example of sharing your experience rather than proclaiming abstract truths or talking about the experiences of other well-known Christians will accelerate this shift from an informational approach to a formational process. Trust that the Holy Spirit will indeed help group members to see or hear what they really need. You may offer what you consider a great insight to which no one responds. If it is what the group needs, the Spirit will bring it around again at a more opportune time. Susan Muto, a modern writer on spiritual formation, often says that we need to "make space for the pace of grace." There are no shortcuts to spiritual growth. Be patient and trust the Spirit.

Listening is another critical quality for a leader of a spiritual formation group. This does not mean simply listening for people to say what you hope they will say so that you can jump in and reinforce them. You need to listen for what is actually going on. What is actually happening in participants' minds and hearts may differ greatly from what you expect after reading the material and doing the weekly exercises yourself. While you listen, you might jot down brief notes about themes that emerge in the discussion. Does a particular type of experience seem to be at the center of the sharing? Is a certain direction or common understanding emerging—a hint of God's will or a shared sense of what was especially helpful to several members of the group? Is there some action that group members need to take together or individually in order to move forward or to respond to an emerging sense of call? What do you hear again and again?

A group leader also needs to be accepting. Accept that group members may have had spiritual experiences quite unlike yours and that people often see common experiences in different ways. Some may be struck by an aspect that you found unimpressive, while others may be left cold by dimensions that really excite or move you. As you model acceptance, you will help foster acceptance of differences within the group. Beyond accepting differences, you will need to accept lack of closure. Group meetings will rarely tie up all the loose ends in a neat package. Burning questions will be left hanging. If important, they will surface again (which brings us back to patience and trust). Also be prepared to accept people's emotions along with their thoughts and experiences. Tears, fears, joy, and anger are to be received as legitimate responses along this journey. One important expression of acceptance is permission-giving. Permit people to grow and share at their own pace. Let group members know in your first meeting that while you want to encourage full participation in every part of the process, they are free to "opt out" of anything that makes them feel truly uncomfortable. No one will be forced to share or pray without consent. "Where the Spirit of the Lord is, there is freedom" (2 Cor. 3:17).

It is particularly important to avoid three common tendencies:

1. *Fixing.* When someone presents a specific problem, you may be tempted to want to find a solution and "fix" the problem. Problem solving generally makes us feel better. Perhaps it makes us feel wise or powerful or helps to break the tension, but it will not help the other to grow. Moreover, you might prescribe the wrong fix. If you have faced a similar problem, speak rather about your own experience and what worked for you. If you have not had direct experience, perhaps someone else in the group has.

2. *Proselytizing.* You know what has brought you closer to God. Naturally you would like everyone to try it. You can offer your own experience to the group, but trying to convince everyone to follow your path is spiritually dangerous. Here is where your knowledge and wisdom come into play. Teresa of Ávila wrote that if she had to choose between a director who was spiritual or one who was learned, she would pick the learned one. The saint might be able to talk only about his or her own spiritual path. The learned one might at least recognize another person's experience from having read about such experiences. Clarifying and celebrating someone else's experience is far more useful than urging others to try to follow your way.

3. *Controlling.* Many of us are accustomed to filling in silence with comment. We may be tempted to see ourselves as experts with an appropriate response to whatever anyone says; that is, we tend to dominate and control the conversation. Here again patience and listening are essential. Do not be afraid of silence. Your capacity to be comfortable with silence allows you to be a relaxed presence in the group. If you really cannot bear a long silence, break it with an invitation for someone (maybe someone who has been quiet so far) to share a thought, feeling, or question rather than with a comment of your own.

If this style of leadership seems challenging or unfamiliar to you, please seriously consider attending a leader training event for *Companions in Christ.* While leadership training is not required to use this resource, it is highly recommended and strongly encouraged.

Expectations for the "Opening" and "Sharing Insights" Sections of Each Meeting

This section offers a basic process for the first hour of your group session. The first step in the group session is prayer and a time of quiet centering. Invoking the Holy Spirit's guiding presence is especially important in the "Opening," or gathering, portion of the weekly group meeting (see "A General Outline of Each Group meeting," pages 19–21).

Most of the "Sharing Insights" part of the group session will focus on individual members talking about their experiences with the daily exercises. Members should bring their journals to refresh their memories of the week's exercises. As the leader, you will generally want to model by beginning with your own sharing, which sets the tone for the rest of the group. Make your sharing brief (two to three minutes) in order to allow ample time for others to share. Above all make the sharing specific, dealing with your response to one of the exercises. You need not announce a general topic. The rest of the group will have read the material and done the exercises. If your sharing is general or abstract, other participants will be less likely to share personal experiences. Your initial sharing in this part of the group meeting is one of your most important roles as a leader. Consider carefully each week what you would like to share, remaining mindful of the role of your sharing in establishing trust in the group as well as the serious intent of this part of the meeting.

During the "Sharing Insights" time, your main job is to listen. Listen primarily for themes—similar experiences that suggest a general truth about the spiritual life, common responses to the readings that might indicate a word God wants the group to hear, or recurring experiences that might offer practical help to other group members as they try to hear and respond to God's call. Take simple notes so you can lift up these themes as the

"Sharing Insights" time comes to an end. You will also invite the other group members to share any themes or patterns they may have identified from the discussion. Listen too for key differences in participants' experiences and affirm the variety of ways God speaks to and guides each one of us. Be alert to participants' temptation to "fix" problems, control conversation, or proselytize. Gently remind them to share only their own experiences or reactions. The same guidance applies if a participant mentions someone else as an example, whether in the group or outside it. Nothing can destroy group trust more quickly than exposing confidences.

By establishing up front some ground rules for group sharing, you may avoid problems. In the Preparatory Meeting, you will explain the various components of each week's meeting. Discuss the nature of this sharing time and establish some basic ground rules for the group. Here are some suggestions:

- Speak only for yourself about beliefs, feelings, and responses.

- Respect and receive what others offer, even if you disagree.

- Listening is more important than talking. Avoid cross talk, interrupting, speaking for others, or trying to "fix" another person's problems.

- Honor the different ways God works in individuals.

- Do not be afraid of silence. Use it to listen to the Spirit in your midst.

- Maintain confidentiality. What is shared in the group stays in the group.

- Recognize that all group members have permission to share only what and when they are ready to share.

You may want to add to this list before you share it with the group.

A few minutes before the scheduled end of the group sharing session, state aloud any themes you have noted during the discussion: a summary report on what you have heard, not a chance to "get in the last word" on various discussion topics. Make it fairly brief: "I noticed that several of us were drawn to a particular passage. I wonder if God is trying to call our attention to something here." This is a time for summarizing and tying together some themes that have already surfaced.

Finally, you may want to close this part of the session with prayer for the deepening of particular insights, for the ability to follow through on the themes or guidance you have heard, for God's leading on questions that have been left open, or for particular situations that have been mentioned. And you may want to invite all group members who are willing to offer simple sentence prayers of their own.

A General Outline of Each Group Meeting

The weekly group meetings will typically follow the outline explained below. Within the outline are two overall movements: one emphasizes sharing insights and learnings from the week's reading and daily exercises; the other develops a deeper understanding of spiritual disciplines or practices. The first movement, called "Sharing Insights," is a time of sharing and listening as described in the preceding section. Sometimes, particularly in the beginning, a more structured approach will be necessary. The second part of the meeting, called "Deeper Explorations," may expand on ideas contained in the week's reading, offer practice in spiritual exercises taught in the reading, or give group members a chance to reflect on the implications of what they learn for their own journeys and for the church. It may include a brief look forward if special preparation is needed for the coming week.

Both movements are intended as times for formation. The first focuses on the group members' responses to the weekly reading and exercises. The second focuses on expanding and deepening the content of the reading.

Consider carefully the setting for your group meetings. An adaptable space is important for group process. One helpful arrangement is a circle of comfortable chairs or sofas. Or participants might want a surface for writing or drawing. Since the group will sometimes break into pairs or triads, space to separate is also important. The space for meeting will need to be relatively quiet and peaceful.

A visual focus for the group is important, especially for opening and closing worship times. Some weeks you are free to create this focus in whatever way you choose, perhaps simply with a candle on a small table in the center of the circle.

OPENING (10 MINUTES)

This brief time of worship will give group members a chance to quiet down and prepare for the group session to follow. Each group will eventually discover what works best for its members. The Leader's Guide offers some specific suggestions, but you can develop your own pattern of prayer and centering, if you desire. Possibilities for this opening worship include (1) singing a hymn together, or listening to a selected song on tape or CD; (2) silence; (3) lighting a candle; (4) scripture or other reading; (5) individual prayer, planned or extemporaneous; or (6) group prayer using a written or memorized prayer.

SHARING INSIGHTS (45 MINUTES)

The content for this part of the meeting comes from the weekly reading and from participants' responses to the five daily exercises they have completed since the last meeting. If members fail to read the material or skip the daily exercises, they will be left out. If too many come unprepared, the group process simply will not work. Group discussion generally will follow the model given above under "Expectations for the 'Opening' and 'Sharing Insights' Sections of Each Meeting." Since the "Opening" has provided prayer and centering time, this section begins with sharing from you as the group leader, continues with group interaction, and ends with summary you feel is helpful, followed by a brief prayer. You will need to keep an eye on the time in order to bring the sharing to a close and have time for the summary and prayer.

BREAK (10 MINUTES)

Group break time serves important physical, mental, and relational purposes. It also gives some time for snacking if you arrange for someone to provide food. Do not neglect adequate break time, and be sure to take a break yourself as leader.

DEEPER EXPLORATIONS (45 MINUTES)

This part of the group meeting builds on material in the weekly reading and daily exercises. The content is designed to help group members explore in greater depth the weekly theme, generally through scriptural meditation, prayer, creative process, personal reflection, and sharing. This segment of the meeting is quite important, resembling the experiential part of a spiritual retreat in miniature and requiring your thoughtful preparation if you are to guide the process comfortably. Please review the leader material early in the week prior to the meeting so that you have time to think through the process and complete any preparation.

CLOSING (10 MINUTES)

As it began, the group meeting ends with a brief time of worship. First you may need to attend to practical matters of meeting place or provision of refreshments if these vary from week to week. You may also have the group draw names for prayer partners for the coming week and ask for prayer requests.

The Leader's Guide includes specific suggestions for the "Closing." Designed to follow closely from the "Deeper Explorations," they may include symbolic acts or rituals of celebration and commitment.

Concluding Matters

Song or hymn selections for the "Opening" and "Closing" times need careful consideration. Review the hymnals or songbooks available to you, and look for singable tunes with thematically appropriate words. If your group sings reluctantly, get several audiocassette tapes or CDs to play and invite "sing-alongs."

In addition to traditional hymns and contemporary praise songs, a newer repertoire of contemplative song and chant is emerging from communities such as Taizé and Iona. Some of these newer pieces may be found in *The Faith We Sing* (TFWS), an ecumenical and international songbook published by Abingdon Press as a supplement to *The United Methodist Hymnal*. Iona Community songs, also ecumenical and international in scope, can be found or ordered through many religious bookstores.

The Leader's Guide occasionally suggests songs for certain meetings, but they are suggestions only. Each group will have access to different hymnals and songbooks and may have its own preference in musical style. The Participant's Book (pages 118–19) includes a song written specifically for *Companions in Christ* called "Companion Song." It includes annotations both for piano and guitar accompaniment. The music is easy to learn, and the song could serve as a theme song for your group. We encourage you to try it in your Preparatory Meeting and to use it several times during the early meetings. If the group likes it, participants will naturally ask to sing it as you move through these weeks together.

The purpose of the Companions in Christ series is to equip persons of faith with both personal and corporate spiritual life practices that will continue long beyond the time frame of this particular resource. Participants may continue certain disciplines on their own or carry some practices into congregational life. Others may desire the continuation of a small group. You will likely discover, as you guide your group through this journey, that certain topics generate interest and energy for further exploration. Some group members may wish that certain readings or weekly meetings could go into more depth. When the group expresses strong desire to continue with a particular topic or practice, take special note of it. A number of possibilities exists for small-group study and practice beyond this resource. Some suggested resources are listed on pages 105–111 of the Participant's Book. The group will need to decide future directions toward the end of this experience.

Our prayer for you as a leader is that the weeks ahead will lead you and your group deeper into the way of life that witnesses to God's reign. May your companionship with Christ and with one another be richly blessed!

Preparatory Meeting

The Leader's Guide to *Companions in Christ: The Way of Blessedness* addresses you, the leader, directly as it presents the material for each group meeting. In places the Leader's Guide offers suggested words for you to speak to the group as a way of introducing various sections. Where this occurs, the words are printed in a bold typeface (such as the first item under "Set the Context"). These words are only suggestions. Always feel free to express the same idea in your own words or adapt it as you deem necessary.

When you are instructed to guide a reflection process, you will often see ellipses (…). These marks indicate pauses between your words to allow participants to ponder them. You will need to develop your own sense of timing in relation to the overall time frame for that portion of the meeting. Generally 15 to 30 seconds are sufficient for each pause.

The content of the Leader's Guide assumes that groups are new to the Companions in Christ resources and provides complete explanations of all aspects of the journey. For example, in the Preparatory Meeting participants carefully review the daily and weekly rhythm and are introduced to the printed resource. If your entire group has experienced *Companions*, feel free to abbreviate familiar material and focus on the distinctive nature of this resource and your group's acquaintance process. You may also choose to skip over the "Holy Listening" exercise and move directly to the "Closing," although a review of deep listening can be valuable even for an experienced group.

PREPARATION

Prepare yourself spiritually. Review the section called "Introduction to *Companions in Christ*" in the Participant's Book, as well as the Introduction in the Leader's Guide. Look over the Contents page in the Participant's Book so that you can answer basic questions about topics. Pray for each group member and for the beginning of this journey together as companions in Christ. Also pray that God will guide you in your role as leader so that the small group might begin this time together with openness and genuine expectation.

Prepare materials and meeting space. Make sure you have a copy of the Participant's Book for each person. You will need a marker and newsprint or other large piece of paper with group ground rules written out in advance on it; a printout from *The Way of Blessedness* groups area of the Web site, www.companionsinchrist.org, that lists groups with whom you may choose to partner; and the card "Prayer for Our Companions in Christ Groups" (in the back of this Leader's Guide). If you are using the listening exercise in the Preparatory Meeting, you will also need copies of the handouts titled "Holy Listening Exercise" and "Review Questions." Arrange for hymnals or songbooks. Select the hymns or songs you will use in the "Opening" and "Closing."

Set chairs in a circle around a center table with a Christ candle. Make your meeting space inviting and visually attractive.

Review the intent of this meeting: to gain a clear grasp of the purpose and process of *Companions in Christ: The Way of Blessedness*, to have the opportunity to express questions and hopes concerning this journey, and to review and adopt group ground rules to observe.

OPENING (10 MINUTES)

Welcome all participants as they enter, and introduce yourself.

Set the context.

- This meeting will prepare us to participate in a new venture called *Companions in Christ: The Way of Blessedness*.

- This small-group experience in spiritual formation guides us through the Beatitudes. In these teachings, Jesus shows us the nature of the blessed life and invites us to practice living within the reign of God.

- As we journey together, we will listen for new ways of hearing Jesus' call to be disciples—as individuals and as a small group.

Introduce ourselves.

- Invite participants to introduce themselves by saying their name and a few words about what drew them to this group. Encourage honest sharing and attentive listening.

- As leader, model by introducing yourself first. Encourage others to follow you.

Join together in worship.

- Invite the group into a time of worship before discussing other matters.

- Light a candle as a symbol of Christ's presence in your midst. Say words like these: **We light this candle to remind us of Christ's presence, guidance, and blessing enfolding us as we begin this journey.**

- Tell the group that one simple definition of blessedness is "awareness of God's presence." Ask participants to take a moment of quiet to recall a time during the past week when they have experienced blessedness in this sense. Awareness of divine presence might have come in joy, trial, or an ordinary moment.

- Ask them to find a single word that represents that experience of blessedness and to note it in their journal.

- After a minute, encourage members to share their word aloud. As leader, begin by sharing your word.

- Conclude with a spontaneous prayer or with these words: **Gracious God, as we journey through *The Way of Blessedness*, open our hearts that we might be aware of your presence with us step-by-step. In Jesus' name. Amen.**

PRESENT THE RESOURCES AND GROUP PROCESS (10 MINUTES)

Make sure each participant has a copy of the Participant's Book. Go over the content with group members so that each person understands the process of reading, daily exercises, and journaling, as well as the outline for each group meeting. Here are some items you will want to mention:

Basic flow of the week. Each participant reads the article for the week on Day 1 (the day after the group meeting) and works through the five daily exercises over Days 2 through 6. The group meets on Day 7. Encourage participants' faithfulness to the process. In preparation for the group meeting, suggest that after Exercise 5 they read over their notebook or journal entries for that week.

Basic flow of a group meeting. Explain the various components: "Opening" (similar to our opening worship time), "Sharing Insights," "Deeper Explorations," and "Closing." Summarize for the group the explanatory material found in "A General Outline of Each Group Meeting" on pages 19–21 of the Introduction in this Leader's Guide.

Materials for each meeting. Ask the members to bring their Bible, Participant's Book, and journal to each meeting. Because use of the Bible is part of the daily exercises, encourage them to use a favorite modern translation.

EXPLAIN PARTICIPANT RESPONSIBILITIES (15 MINUTES)

Emphasize the importance of each member's commitment to the daily exercises and practices in making the group process work. Because some members will not have experienced this type of daily reflection or group interaction, they may need help in feeling comfortable with them. Remind participants that one of the ways we listen to God is by putting our experiences into words. Throughout the week, we record these experiences in our journal. In the group meeting, we articulate our recorded experiences. Both processes bring clarity and new perspective.

Present the process of journaling.
Note that participants may already be exercising an important practice for the course: journaling. Call their attention to pertinent points from the material on pages 12–13 of the Participant's Book about the value of recording reflections in a journal or personal notebook. Assure them that the writing can be as informal and unstructured as they want. Because each person keeps notes that are most helpful for him or her, the journal becomes the personal record of the spiritual growth that this resource is designed to encourage.

Consider the commitment of listening.
Another important commitment group members make is to listen to and value the words of others. As companions together, we give full attention to what God is doing in the life of the one speaking. We learn to listen with our heart as well as our head and to create an accepting space in which all can freely explore their spiritual journeys. The group becomes a place for deep listening and trusting in God's guiding presence.

Discuss Common Ground Rules (15 minutes)

Ground rules are explained fully on page 18 in the Introduction to this Leader's Guide. The rules suggested in the Introduction should prove helpful, but as leader you should be prepared to offer other rules appropriate to the group. You will also want to allow members to make suggestions. Write the completed list on newsprint for the group to see. Remember that the goal is not a formal agreement or covenant but recognition of the basic rules that are essential in order for the group to deepen its faith and mature as a community.

Introduce the *Companions in Christ* Network and Prayer Connections (5 minutes)

Although we focus on what is happening in our group, we remember that many other groups across the country are participating in *Companions in Christ* also. We can communicate with those groups who are on the same spiritual journey in ways that strengthen our bonds in the body of Christ. We have two opportunities to connect with others:

- *Correspondence with other groups.* Look for the link to *The Way of Blessedness* groups on the *Companions in Christ* Web site (www.companionsinchrist.org). Print out a list of the groups with whom you might partner. You can search for a group by city, state, country, denomination, or other key words. While at the site, add your group to the list so that it is available to others looking for a partner. Encourage your members to select and partner with a group, perhaps communicating through notes of greeting and encouragement, or by sending a small love-gift. Use the preparatory meeting as a time to determine how you will proceed with this partnership. You might ask for a volunteer to guide its development.

- The Upper Room Living Prayer Center and its network of prayer volunteers will begin to hold your group in prayer. Simply fill in and mail the card titled "Prayers for Our *Companions in Christ* Group" that is bound into the Leader's Guide. Complete the leader's portion of the card by providing your name and your church's mailing address. Please do not use a post office box number. Ask each member of the group to sign his or her first name as evidence of the group's desire to be connected to the larger network of persons involved in *Companions in Christ.*

Note to leaders: If your whole group has already experienced *Companions in Christ* and is familiar with the practice of holy listening, you may choose to proceed directly to the

"Closing." Do consider, however, the value of allowing participants to experience this centrally important exercise again. The practice of holy listening is always fruitful.

BREAK (10 MINUTES)

DEEPER EXPLORATIONS (45 MINUTES)

Introduce the "Holy Listening Exercise." (5 minutes)

- This exercise will give everyone a chance to practice prayerful or holy listening, the heart of spiritual friendship and an important element in formational experiences such as *Companions in Christ.* This listening practice is essential to all formational settings: formal or informal, one-on-one, or in a group.

- Ask the group members to pair up for the exercise.

- Give everyone the "Holy Listening Exercise" and "Review Questions" handouts. Explain the process to the group.

- Assure participants that each person will have the opportunity to be both a listener and a speaker. After the first eight minutes, they will take two minutes to reflect on the review questions. Then they will trade roles. At the end of the second eight-minute session, they again take two minutes to reflect quietly with the review questions. During the last five minutes they will compare their responses to the review questions.

Practice holy listening in pairs. (25 minutes)

- Ask pairs to find a space apart quickly in order to make the most of the time.

- Help participants honor the time by ringing a bell or calling out the time after each eight-minute period and by reminding them to take two minutes to reflect on the review questions. Alert the participants at the close of the two minutes of reflection time to change roles.

- After the second listening session and evaluation, encourage each pair to compare notes on the experience for five minutes.

Gather as a group. (5 minutes)

- Call pairs together as a total group to share what they have learned about holy listening.

Close with this affirmation of the exercise: **There is no greater gift one person can give to another than to listen intently.**

CLOSING (10 MINUTES)

Introduce the option of an additional week for sharing spiritual journeys after Week 1 (see Introduction, page 13). Briefly name the benefits of sharing spiritual journeys with one another. Be sure participants understand that there is no article to read. Instead there are six questions to guide daily reflection and journaling. These reflections aid the sharing process in the next weekly meeting. Tell the group members that they will decide at the end of the next meeting whether to add a week for sharing their spiritual journeys. Ask them to think and pray about it until then.

Invite a time of quiet reflection. **What are your hopes for the time ahead of us as companions in Christ?…What are your anxieties about these next weeks together?…Commit both your hopes and fears to God now in silent prayer.…**

Offer a brief word of prayer, asking that all might be able to release their hopes and concerns into God's gracious hands. End with thanksgiving for each person and for God's good purposes in bringing this group together.

Close with song. You may wish to introduce the "Companion Song" to your group (printed on pages 118–119 of the Participant's Book), or choose a favorite hymn.

Remind the members of their weekly assignment. On the first day they will read the article for Week 1, "Exploring the Blessed Life." During each of the next five days they will work through one exercise and record their thoughts in their journal. Be sure all participants know the location and time of the next meeting and any special responsibilities (such as providing snacks or helping to arrange the worship table).

Holy Listening Exercise

"Spiritual direction takes place when two people agree to give their full attention to what God is doing in one (or both) of their lives and seek to respond in faith."[1]

The purpose of this exercise is for participants to practice holy listening in pairs.

As the Speaker

Receive your chance to speak and be heard as an opportunity to explore an aspect of your walk with God during the past week (or day). Remember that you and your friend meet in the company of God, who is the true guiding presence of this time together.

As the Listener

Practice listening with your heart as well as your head. Create a welcoming, accepting space in which the other person may explore freely his or her journey in your presence and in the presence of God. Be natural, but be alert to any habits or anxious needs in you to analyze, judge, counsel, "fix," teach, or share your own experience. Try to limit your speech to gentle questions and honest words of encouragement.

Be inwardly prayerful as you listen, paying attention to the Spirit even as you listen to the holy mystery of the person before you.

When appropriate and unintrusive, invite the other person to explore simple questions such as these:

* Where did you experience God's grace or presence in the midst of this time?

* Do you sense God calling you to take a step forward in faith or love? Is there an invitation here to explore?

How to Begin and End the Conversation

* Decide who will be the first listener, and begin with a moment of silent prayer.

* Converse for eight minutes; then pause for two minutes so that each person may respond to the review questions in silence.

* Trade roles and converse for eight minutes more; then pause again for personal review.

* Use the last five minutes to compare notes on your experiences and your responses to the review questions.

Review Questions

FOR THE LISTENER

a. When were you most aware of God's presence (in you, in the other person, between you) in the midst of the conversation?

b. What interrupted or diminished the quality of your presence to God or to the other person?

c. What was the greatest challenge of this experience for you?

FOR THE SPEAKER

a. What was the gift of the conversation for you?

b. What in the listener's manner helped or hindered your ability to pay attention to your life experience and God's presence in it?

c. When were you most aware of God's presence (in you, in the other person, or between you) in the midst of the conversation?

Week 1

Exploring the Blessed Life

PREPARATION

Prepare yourself spiritually. Pray for each participant and for your ability to be present to the Spirit in this meeting time. Review the material in the Introduction of this Leader's Guide to remind yourself of important elements in small-group spiritual formation and your role as leader. Read the article for Week 1, do all the exercises, and keep your journal.

Prepare materials and the meeting space. In the meeting room, display the ground rules developed at last week's meeting. If you wish to introduce the "Candle Prayer" in today's "Opening," print and display it on newsprint (keep for future meetings). If your group elected to partner with another group, arrange for updates on any progress. You will also need to write on newsprint the following scripture references: Genesis 12:1-2; Numbers 6:24-26; Matthew 16:17; Ephesians 1:3-6; 1 John 3:1-2. Participants will read these aloud from their own Bibles. Also print the two statements for seeking and offering blessings in the "Closing" (pages 37–38). Both the "Sharing Insights" time and the "Closing" require blank newsprint and a marker. Arrange chairs in a circle or around a table. Place a candle at the center of the circle or table. If you have a partner group, consider placing a symbol near the candle that represents your commitment to pray for and support its members. Make sure hymnals or songbooks are available. Select songs for the "Opening" and "Closing." Be prepared to hand out copies of the sheet titled "Sharing Spiritual Journeys, Questions for Daily Reflection and Journaling" (page 40), if the group chooses the option of an additional weekly meeting for sharing spiritual journeys.

Review the intent of this meeting: to discover where we are in our walk with Christ and to hear the call to enter the way of blessedness.

OPENING (10 MINUTES)

Welcome all participants by name as they enter.

Set a context.

This meeting is designed to help us listen to the blessing and call of Christ in the Beatitudes. It is an opportunity to explore for ourselves what it means to live "the way of blessedness." This part of the meeting gives us time to share from our daily practice, our progress or difficulties, and to reflect together on insights.

Join together in worship.

- Light the candle at the center of the group. As you do so acknowledge Christ's presence, offering words such as these: **We light this candle to remind us of Christ's presence in our midst.** Or invite the group to recite in unison the "Candle Prayer."

- Invite participants to relax and let the words of scripture flow over them as you read a passage. Let them know that no discussion will follow the reading, so they can simply open their hearts and absorb God's word.

- Read Ephesians 1:3-6 at an unhurried pace, followed by a minute or so of silence.

  Blessed be the God and Father of our Lord Jesus Christ, who has blessed us in Christ with every spiritual blessing in the heavenly places, just as he chose us in Christ before the foundation of the world to be holy and blameless before him in love. He destined us for adoption as his children through Jesus Christ, according to the good pleasure of his will, to the praise of his glorious grace that he freely bestowed on us in the Beloved.

- Read the following quote from Lloyd John Ogilvie, allowing a moment after for quiet reflection:

  To be a blessed person is to know, feel, and relish God's affirmation and assurance, acceptance, and approval. It is the experience of being chosen and cherished, valued and enjoyed.[1]

- Offer a prayer of your choosing or use these words: **God of glory, may we receive the immense grace of your blessing to us in Christ Jesus, and learn from him how to live the blessed life that is the pathway into your kingdom. In his name we pray. Amen.**

- Sing a favorite hymn or "Blest Are They" (*The Faith We Sing*).

SHARING INSIGHTS (45 MINUTES)

You and members of your group will share your insights and experiences of God's presence in your lives this past week. Begin by reminding everyone of the theme for the week—exploring the blessed life.

1. Ask participants to take the next five minutes to review the article and their journal entries from the week. Ask them to pay particular attention to their reflections on Exercise 4 (Matthew 5:1-10). (*5 minutes*)

2. Invite group members to share insights from the week's reading and Exercise 4. (See the Leader's Notes on page 38.) Model the sharing by offering your brief reflections first. If you have time, ask the group to share responses to Exercise 5 also. (*35 minutes*)

3. Conclude by identifying the main points or common themes that emerged from the sharing. What themes occurred more than once? (*5 minutes*)

BREAK (10 MINUTES)
During the break you will need to post the scripture references you have listed on newsprint.

DEEPER EXPLORATIONS (45 MINUTES)

Invite the participants to explore the nature of God's blessing and begin listening to what Jesus wants to say to them through the Beatitudes.

Initiate a conversation on the nature of blessing. (10 minutes)

- Ask several persons to read aloud from their own Bibles, at a leisurely pace, the passages listed on newsprint. After each reading, allow a quiet pause to ponder what it says about the nature of God's blessing.

- Invite prayerful sharing.

- If necessary, bring out the point that God has already blessed us with "every spiritual blessing in the heavenly places" in Jesus Christ. Divine blessing is not something we can wrest from God or earn by being good. The way of blessedness begins with accepting God's blessing of a new life in Christ.

Set a context for a meditation on the Beatitudes. (3 minutes)

- **The Beatitudes give specific content to God's blessing and the life for which we are blessed. The Participant's Book suggests that in these eight statements Jesus "portrays the character of the citizen of the kingdom of God." Together the dispositions found in the Beatitudes describe what Jesus calls us to be and become as we follow him.**

- *The Way of Blessedness* is an opportunity to explore the Beatitudes as a pathway of spiritual formation, a "rule of life" for Christian disciples who would become citizens of

God's realm. They are not eight different blessings but one blessing seen from eight angles, the blessedness of belonging to the kingdom.

Guide an exercise with Matthew 5:1-10. (15 minutes)

We are going to observe a quiet time now to listen deeply to Matthew 5:1-10. Hear the reading not as an observer but as a participant in the scene, someone to whom Jesus is speaking. Open yourself to receive God's blessing for who you already are and how you are called to grow as a follower of Christ.

Read verses 1-10 aloud at a relaxed pace.

Pause, then encourage the group to listen more deeply as you read the text again. After reading verses 1 and 2, ask the participants to find themselves in the scene, as one of the twelve disciples or as another follower listening to Jesus' words on the hillside.

Invite them, as you continue reading, to pay attention to the beatitude that especially touches them or claims their attention in a special way today.

Read verses 3-10 again. Ask the participants to spend a few minutes pondering the verse that draws them, exploring its meaning or importance. Suggest that they paraphrase the beatitude as a way of connecting with it more deeply.

Now read the following meditation aloud, pausing where indicated(…), to guide the reflection process:

What do Jesus' words in this beatitude mean to you personally?…

Imagine now taking a walk around the hillside on the mount where Jesus has been teaching. As you walk you ponder the mystery of what you have just heard.… What question would you really like to ask about this beatitude or about the life Jesus is calling you to or about the life you now live?…

As you walk, you round a curve on the hill. And there is Jesus before you.… As you look into his eyes, allow yourself to feel the warmth with which you are received and welcomed into his presence.…

Jesus says, "What would you ask of me?"…

Ask him your question, and listen for his response.…

Take in his response.…

Now he blesses you and sends you on your way. What blessing does he give you?…How does it meet your need?…

Take time to journal and pray. (10 minutes)

Give the participants a few minutes to record impressions and insights in their journals. Then invite them to write a simple prayer that expresses their desire to grow spiritually, the obstacles they face, and the grace they need to live more fully the blessed life.

Gather in pairs or triads to share from reflections. (7 minutes)

- Suggest these questions to guide the sharing:

   1. What aspect of the beatitude you chose beckons to you?

   2. What grace would you ask the other(s) to pray for in your life as you begin this small group journey?

- Invite them to enter a minute of silent prayer for one another in pairs or triads.

Closing (**10 minutes**)

Read this passage from Ephesians 3:16-19, Paul's prayer for God's deep blessing upon the church community at Ephesus. Offer it as a blessing to the group:

> I pray that, according to the riches of his glory, he may grant that you may be strengthened in your inner being with power through his Spirit, and that Christ may dwell in your hearts through faith, as you are being rooted and grounded in love. I pray that you may have the power to comprehend, with all the saints, what is the breadth and length and height and depth, and to know the love of Christ that surpasses knowledge, so that you may be filled with all the fullness of God.

Name the power of blessing. **To bless one another is actually to convey God's blessing through our intentions and words. A blessing is not just a pleasant sentiment. It carries the power of God's grace to another person through the action of the Holy Spirit.**

Identify the blessing each seeks. Refer to the two statements you have printed on newsprint or a board. Give the participants a minute to reflect on the first one and to fill in the blank:

"As I begin to live the way of blessedness, I desire the blessing of _____."

Invite the group members to speak their completed sentences around the circle. In response, the group will offer a blessing to each person by name, saying:

"God bless you, (Susan), with the gift of _____ . In Jesus' name. Amen."

Sing a song of blessing. Suggestion: "Bless the Lord My Soul" (TFWS)

Offer the following paraphrase (or your own version) of the familiar benediction from Numbers 6:24-26. Note for the group that *benediction* means "good word" and is a synonym for blessing.

> May the Lord be with you and watch over you.
> May the Lord smile on you and graciously receive you as you are.
> May the Lord's smile shine through you to others
> and make you to be God's peace wherever you are.

Gather consensus of the group on the option for an additional weekly meeting (next week) to share spiritual journeys with one another. If the group agrees, hand out the sheet for daily reflection ("Sharing Spiritual Journeys, Questions for Daily Reflection and Journaling," page 40) and clarify the time frame for each person's sharing in the next meeting.

Leader's Notes

Gather participants' responses to Exercise 4 on a board or newsprint. The columns might look something like this; however, they need not be equivalent on both sides.

What Culture Blesses	What God Blesses
Wealth, having it all together, no need unmet	Simplicity, surrender, dependence on God
Being "cool," impervious to feeling, in control	Vulnerability, tears, humility
Power of domination, influence of force	Gentleness, strength of clarity, power of truth
Status quo satisfaction, greed, deception	Justice, love of the good and the right
Revenge, reprisal, legalism	Tenderheartedness, forgiveness
People pleasing, multiplicity, divided attentions	Singleness of purpose, God-focused unity
Apathy, self-centeredness, exciting tension	Reconciliation, harmony, shalom
Conflict avoidance, scapegoating hostility	Courage, perseverance, bravery in love

---

Optional Session for Sharing Spiritual Journeys

OPENING (5 MINUTES)

Welcome all participants personally as they enter.

Set a context.

- **Before we begin our journey through the Beatitudes, we will tell something of the stories of our personal journeys to help us grow together as a Christian community.**

- Remind the group members of how much time each one has to share his or her story.

Join together in worship.

- Light a candle to signal God's presence in our midst.

- Ask participants to listen as you read Deuteronomy 26:5-9 (begin with "A wandering Aramean…"). This is one of the Bible's earliest stories about the spiritual journey of the Israelite people and the guidance of God.

- Pause to give silent thanks for God's guiding presence on our spiritual journeys.

SHARING SPIRITUAL JOURNEYS (1 HOUR AND 50 MINUTES, INCLUDING BREAK)

As leader be the first to share your journey, modeling the sharing for others. Be sure to observe the time limit established for the group members.

CLOSING (5 MINUTES)

- Invite the group to form a circle and join hands as you offer a sentence prayer of thanksgiving or intercession for each person in turn.

- Lead the group in a few minutes of prayerful reflection on the experience of listening and presenting our stories. **What were you aware of as you listened? as you presented? Where did you hear or see God in one another's stories?**

Offer a closing prayer, or sing a benediction. Suggestion: "I Was There to Hear Your Borning Cry" (TFWS)

Optional Week: Sharing Spiritual Journeys
Questions for Daily Reflection and Journaling

Spend time pondering one question each day. Then write a response in two or three sentences, capturing the central ideas or images from your reflection time. These responses will help guide and focus your sharing in the next small group meeting.

1. Describe your image of God when you were a child. What shaped that image? What is your image of God now? What has influenced changes in your image of God?

2. Name three people who have most influenced your spiritual growth over your lifetime. How have you known God's grace and blessing through them? What, in a word or phrase, did you learn from each one?

3. Identify three significant turning points in your life, defining moments that have shaped your identity and beliefs. If you have come to understand God's guiding purpose and grace in these experiences, record your insights in your journal.

4. When have you known the greatest sense of God's blessing in your life? Have you ever felt a sense of God's absence? Describe these experiences in your journal.

5. For what do you deeply hunger in your spiritual life? How have you become aware of your spiritual hungers?

6. To what do you feel most firmly committed in your spiritual life? How would you name the grace and the challenge of these commitments?

Week 2
Embracing Our Spiritual Poverty

PREPARATION

Prepare yourself spiritually. Since this beatitude is so foundational, pray with particular focus for each participant and for your group meeting. Read the article for Week 2, reflect on each of the daily exercises, and record your responses in your journal.

Prepare materials and the meeting space. Have on hand your group's ground rules, the "Candle Prayer" if you are using it, and any current information about your partner group. Each participant will need a copy of the "Closed Hands, Open Hands" meditation (page 45). Arrange chairs in a circle or around a table. Place a candle at the center of the circle or table. Make sure hymnals or songbooks are available, and select songs for the "Opening" and "Closing."

Review the intent of this meeting: to gain a deeper understanding of being poor in spirit and to practice coming before God with open hands.

OPENING (10 MINUTES)

Welcome all participants personally as they enter.

Set a context.

Welcome to our meeting on the way of blessedness. Today we will explore Jesus' words "Blessed are the poor in spirit..." and what it means to embrace our poverty of spirit as a blessing.

Join together in worship.

- Light the candle as a sign that Christ is in our midst to illumine scripture and open our hearts to wisdom for this journey.

- Read Psalm 113:1-8. In the moments of silence after, repeat verses 7-8.

- Invite sentence prayers from the group. You might begin by modeling a simple prayer such as the following or end the prayer time with it: **Generous God, help us to trust you enough to accept your blessing. Amen.**

  (Note: If your group has a partner group, remember the partners in prayer.)

- Sing a song of your choosing. Suggestions: "Day by Day" or "Change My Heart, O God" (TFWS)

SHARING INSIGHTS (45 MINUTES)

You and the group members will share insights and experiences of God's presence in your lives this past week. Begin by reminding the group of the theme for this week—poverty of spirit as our radical dependence on God.

1. Give the participants time to review the article for this week and their journal entries for the daily exercises. (*5 minutes*)

2. Invite the sharing of insights. As leader, model the sharing by offering your own brief reflections first. Encourage deep and active listening. If the group numbers more than eight, you may want to form two smaller groups to ensure that everyone has the opportunity to share. (*35 minutes*)

3. With the whole group, note any common themes that emerged. **What common themes emerged that might indicate the Spirit's movement in our midst?** (*5 minutes*)

BREAK (10 MINUTES)

DEEPER EXPLORATIONS (45 MINUTES)

Invite participants into a time of prayerful openness and meditation on scripture to deepen their understanding of "poor in spirit."

Introduce the theme. (5 minutes)

In the first beatitude, Jesus names our poverty of spirit as a blessing, calling us to an inward posture of open receptivity to the life God would give us in Christ.

Read the following quote from the late Henri Nouwen. Invite participants, as they listen, to ponder the image of open hands in relation to our spiritual poverty.

To pray means to open your hands before God. It means slowly relaxing the tension which squeezes your hands together and accepting your existence with an increasing readiness, not as a possession to defend, but as a gift to receive. Above all, therefore, prayer is a way of life which allows you to find a stillness in the midst of the world where you open your hands to God's promises, and find hope for yourself, your [fellows] and the whole community in which you live.[1]

Guide the "Closed Hands, Open Hands" meditation. (25 minutes)

Indicate that you and the participants are going to practice opening your hands before God and trusting your lives to God's grace. Invite participants to close their eyes and open their hands before God in a gesture of receptive prayer.

Guide the meditation as follows, at an unhurried pace:

*   "To pray means to open your hands before God," Nouwen says. What is it like to come before God with open hands?… In what areas of your life are you ready to come open-handed before God?

*   Nouwen continues, "To pray means to open your hands before God… slowly relaxing the tension which squeezes your hands together.…" Squeeze your hands together to help you feel this closed posture.… What parts of your life are difficult to open in trust before God?… How would you name the tension?…

*   Now listen to the words of Psalm 23. Ponder the images of God's gracious presence and guidance, allowing them to draw you into trusting faith. And as words of assurance help dissolve your tensions, gradually let your hands unfold and open to God.

*   Read Psalm 23 meditatively as the participants reflect on these images.

*   After a pause, read Nouwen's words again: "To pray means… accepting your existence … not as a possession to defend, but as a gift to receive."

*   Ask the group members to listen again to the psalm, inviting them to rest more deeply in a posture of open-handed prayer: **Let the promise and beauty of these words sink in and renew your spirit. God wants to give what is good out of abundant divine love. You can be confident of this. So let the words of the psalm help you relax, release, and receive from God.**

*   Read Psalm 23 again with longer pauses between phrases. Expand on the text or use alternate translations if you choose (see Leader's Notes, page 46).

Reflect individually. (10 minutes)

Invite the participants to spend the next ten minutes in quiet, reflecting on their experience with the aid of the reflection sheet (see "Closed Hands, Open Hands" handout).

Regather as a group. (15 minutes)

- Ask the participants to share from their experience of this meditation, focusing on what they were able to release or to receive as they opened their hands before God.

- Invite them to reflect on their experience of listening to Psalm 23, with emphasis on fresh insight into this familiar psalm or a phrase that especially touched them.

CLOSING (10 MINUTES)

Remind the group that coming before God with open hands is a powerful image of our basic poverty of spirit, our need for God's grace in all things. Learning to open our hands before God is a way to cultivate the spirit of poverty, humility, and trust.

Invite individual prayer. Ask the participants to close their eyes and choose one phrase of Psalm 23 that especially drew them in this time. Instruct them: **Pray with this verse as you open your hands to God.… Create a welcoming space for God as you repeat the words and form the images in your mind.… Be honest about the grace you need, and let yourself receive whatever gift God is pleased to give you…** (allow a few minutes of silence).

Share in pairs. Invite participants to pair up and name in a word or phrase the grace each needs or the gift received in this time of prayer.

Close with prayer. Invite participants to join hands. Remind them that as we release the posture of tension in our hands, they become available not only to receive God's gifts but to reach out freely and generously to one another. Invite prayers of hope, longing, and gratitude.

Sing a benediction, or "Spirit of the Living God."

Closed Hands, Open Hands

To pray means to open your hands before God. It means slowly relaxing the tension which squeezes your hands together and accepting your existence with an increasing readiness, not as a possession to defend, but as a gift to receive. Above all, therefore, prayer is a way of life which allows you to find a stillness in the midst of the world where you open your hands to God's promises, and find hope for yourself, your [fellows] and the whole community in which you live.

—Henri J. M. Nouwen, *With Open Hands*

What was your experience of coming before God with open hands? What feelings accompany this posture of prayer for you?

What was your experience of hands squeezed together? How did you name the tension they held? How did this posture before God feel?

What phrases or images from Psalm 23 helped you experience God's grace more fully?

What were you able to release?

Leader's Notes

When you read Psalm 23 a second time, you might wish to expand on a few phrases, particularly those that pose difficulty to understanding in a modern sense. For example,

The Lord is my shepherd, I shall not want—I shall not be in want, or lack anything needed.

Or you might add a phrase from another translation to expand the meaning. For example,

He leads me beside still waters—the waters of peace;

He restores my soul—renews life within me.

Even though I walk through the darkest valley—the valley of the shadow of death—*I fear no evil.*

And I shall dwell in the house of the Lord my whole life long—forever.

Week 3

Tears As Anguish, Tears As Gift

PREPARATION

Prepare yourself spiritually. Pray for the hidden losses of group members and for their recognition of God's deep comfort during this week. Read the article for Week 3, reflect on each of the daily exercises, and record your responses in your journal.

Prepare materials and the meeting space. Have on hand your group's ground rules, the "Candle Prayer," and any current information about or from your partner group. Make a copy of the handout "Lamenting Our Loss on the Emmaus Road" (page 52) for each group member. Review this exercise so you can clearly describe the process to the group. Gather art supplies such as construction paper, glue, scissors, colored pencils, play dough or clay, and decide where to place these items in the room. Be sure to have a board or newsprint available and a bell or chime. The "Closing" requires chairs in a circle around a smaller table, so you may wish to set up the room this way from the start if it is not customary. You will also need two pieces of pita bread broken in pieces and in a basket, a small cruet of fragrant oil or an "oil button." Have hymnals or songbooks available, and select songs for the "Opening" and "Closing."

Review the intent of this meeting: to discover the blessing of moving from a worldly perspective on loss to mourning with faith and hope in God's comfort.

OPENING (10 MINUTES)

Welcome participants by name as they enter.

Set a context.

Welcome to our *Companions in Christ* meeting. Today we will explore Jesus' words about the blessedness of mourning. Perhaps we can help one another discover more fully the

nature of divine comfort in the midst of our losses as we bring to grief and penitence the resources of our faith and hope.

Join together in worship.

- Light the candle and invite the group to join you in praying the "Candle Prayer." Or offer brief words to welcome Christ, the great comforter, into your gathering.

- Read Psalm 77:1-6, 9, 11-15.

- Invite the participants to take a few minutes to consider the depth of lament contained in this psalm, then to think on the hope and faith it expresses. They might wish to look at the psalm in their own Bibles.

- Hold a time of silent prayer. Suggest that the participants lift up in their hearts those who have suffered loss and are grieving. After a few minutes conclude the silence with words such as: **God of comfort, enfold those who mourn in your strong, gentle embrace and give them peace. In Jesus' name we pray. Amen.**

  If your group has a partner group, remember the partners in your prayer.

- Sing a hymn. Suggestions: "O How He Loves You and Me" or "God Weeps" (TFWS)

SHARING INSIGHTS (45 MINUTES)

Ask the group members to share where they have experienced insight or God's presence this past week, reminding them of this week's theme—divine comfort in the midst of mourning our losses.

1. Instruct participants to review this week's article and their journal entries. (*5 minutes*)

2. Invite them to share their insights. Offer your own brief reflections first. Encourage the group to practice deep and active listening during this time. (*35 minutes*)

3. Take a few minutes to identify any common themes or experiences that might give clues about God's work in our midst. (*5 minutes*)

BREAK (10 MINUTES)

DEEPER EXPLORATIONS (45 MINUTES)

Guide the group in exploring the practice of lament as a way of working through mourning with open hands before the God of all comfort.

Introduce the theme of lament. (3 minutes)

- Ask: **What differences have you observed between those who grieve with faith and those who grieve without faith?**

- Have someone read 1 Thessalonians 4:13. Highlight the phrase, "so that you may not grieve as others do who have no hope." Point out that Christians certainly grieve but not as those "who have no hope." Our hope is anchored in the life, death, and resurrection of Jesus Christ.

- In this beatitude, Jesus affirms that when we mourn before God with open hands, we receive blessing and comfort.

- The Bible gives us a strong, ancient tradition called "lament" for expressing grief with faith and hope. An entire book of the Bible (Lamentations) and about one-third of the Psalms are devoted to it.

Set a context for the practice of lament. (2 minutes)

A book titled *Way to Live* talks about lament as spiritual and emotional therapy when the storm clouds of grief roll in. To lament is to express sorrow out loud. It gives us time and permission to vent anger, deep sadness, or self-blame. As we pour out our grief and anguish in the presence of God, we begin to sense God's nearness and comfort. We can't remove the storms, quiet the thunder, or stop lightning from striking, but we can trust our tears to be the raindrops that release the clouds until rays of sunlight shine through again.[1]

A lament is like a play in three acts.[2] Write these three words on newsprint and explain briefly:

1. *React:* **We argue with God and express our grief with raw emotion.**
2. *Remember:* **Gradually we remember God's help in the past and acknowledge God's presence with us now.**
3. *Restore:* **As our faith and trust in God return, we see our lives anew and give thanks.**

Reflect on the process of lament in the Emmaus Road story. (5 minutes)

- Ask someone to read aloud the Emmaus Road story (Luke 24:13-35).

- Before the reading, invite the group to listen for ways in which the risen Christ helps the two disciples mourn their loss, keeping in mind the three movements of lament.

- After the reading, ask the participants to name what they saw and heard. (See Leader's Notes, page 53.)

Help the participants lament their own loss on the Emmaus Road. (35 minutes)

- Introduce the exercise (*2 minutes*). Hand out the reflection sheet "Lamenting Our Loss on the Emmaus Road" copied from page 52. Describe the process briefly, clarifying that Part 1 is solitary, Part 2 is in pairs, Part 3 is again solitary. Note the time frames for each part.

- Invite the participants to find a walking partner now and to choose art materials (indicate location). Then tell them to find a place to begin the exercise in relative solitude but near their walking partner. Ask them not to walk beyond the range of the bell or chime that will call them back.

Closing (10 minutes)

Call the group together with a bell or chime.

Place the cruet of oil and the pita bread, broken into pieces in a basket, near the candle at the center of the group. If you have an "oil button," place it in your pocket or keep it near at hand.

Lead the group in singing a song of quiet prayerfulness. Suggestions: "Spirit of the Living God"; "I Surrender All"; "Take, O Take Me As I Am" (Iona)

Invite closing reflection. Ask the group members to review their notes from the reflection sheet. Invite them to meditate on the third movement, restored spiritual vision: "Then their eyes were opened…" (v. 31). Guide the reflection (*2 minutes*) with these words: **Let Christ take your experience now, just as he took up the bread…. Let him lift it up to God, bless it, break it, and give it back to you…. What has he given back to you?… What is he opening your eyes to see?… Give thanks for any insight or healing you may have received in this time…. Amen.**

Engage the group in the ritual of bread and oil.

- Pass the basket of pita bread around the circle. Invite everyone to take a piece and pull apart the double layer so that each person has two pieces.

- Explain that one piece of bread represents a good-bye, and the other a hello. The good-bye is the loss they are releasing. The hello is the grace they are invited to receive as they offer their loss to God. Ask the participants to consider how they would name their good-bye and hello in a word or phrase.

- Pass the basket again, inviting the members (if ready) to let go of the good-bye piece by placing it in the basket. If they choose, they can name aloud their good-bye.

- Then stand near the center table and take up the oil cruet or button. Invite each person, one by one, to name the hello aloud—a word or phrase that captures the grace he or she would receive.

- As each person shares, ask him or her to eat the second piece of bread, tasting and digesting the invitation in this hello. Dip your finger in oil, touch the person's forehead and offer a blessing with words like these: "(**Name**), **I anoint you with the oil of gladness that you may accept your hello with joy and know the comfort of those who mourn.**"

Speak Psalm 30:2, 11-12 as a blessing:

> O Lord, my God, I cried to you for help,
>   and you have healed me.
> . . . .
> You have turned my mourning into dancing;
>   you have taken off my sackcloth
>   and clothed me with joy,
> so that my soul may praise you and not be silent.
> O Lord my God, I will give thanks to you forever.

Lamenting Our Loss on the Emmaus Road

BASED ON LUKE 24:13-35

Choose a personal or corporate loss, disappointment, or sense of sin with which to work. With what "death" are you wrestling?

React (v. 17). "What are you discussing with each other while you walk along?" (*15 minutes*)

Listen to Christ's question as an invitation to tell him your story. Walk with him and tell him about the loss, pain, disappointment, or guilt that continues to weigh heavily on you, undermine your faith, or depress your spirit.

Create an expression of your mourning: make a drawing, play dough form, or paper sculpture; write a song, poem, or psalm of lament.

Remember (v. 27). "Then beginning with Moses and all the prophets, he interpreted to them the things about himself in all the scriptures." (*15 minutes*)

Walk with another group member. Be aware that the risen Christ is with you. Share as much of your situation as you are comfortable doing. Help each other listen for connections between your stories and God's story. What scripture passage, experience, or image does Christ bring to mind? Dwell on it and seek its meaning for you.

Restore (v. 31). "Then their eyes were opened...." (*3 minutes*)

Take a few minutes to note reflections in your journal. Where and how is restoration occurring? How has remembrance helped you come to a new understanding, appreciation, or sense of patience with your situation? In what ways does that comfort you?

Leader's Notes

MOVEMENTS OF LAMENT IN THE EMMAUS STORY

1. Luke 24:13-24. The risen Christ asks questions that invite the disciples to express their sorrow and incomprehension. In retelling the story of the past several days, the disciples begin their lament.

2. Luke 24:25-27. With Christ's illuminating guidance through the scriptures, they remember God's promises and plans. The reorientation of faith takes root in their hearts.

3. Luke 24:28-35. Through a familiar symbolic action, the disciples recognize the risen Christ. Their trust and hope are restored as they recover the "faith sense" of all that has happened. They return to the community of faith to tell the full story.

Week 4

The Power of a Clear and Gentle Heart

PREPARATION

Prepare yourself spiritually. Pray that a spirit of clarity and gentle-heartedness may grow in each participant and in the group as a whole. Read the article for Week 4, reflect on the daily exercises, and keep your journal.

Prepare materials and the meeting space. Have available the "Candle Prayer" if you plan to use it and any current information or ideas about your partner group. Arrange chairs in a circle or around a table, with a candle in the center of the arrangement. Make sure hymnals or songbooks are available, and select songs for the "Opening" and "Closing."

Review the intent of the meeting: to seek godly meekness as an alternative stance in the face of worldly power and choose to live by this sign of God's reign.

OPENING (10 MINUTES)

Welcome all participants by name as they enter.

Set a context.

Today we take another step in our journey through the Beatitudes. We will consider the meaning of true meekness as a serious alternative to worldly power.

Join together in worship.

*   Light the candle and invite the group to join you in the "Candle Prayer." Or offer words such as these: **The warm glow of this candle reminds us of the gentle nature of Jesus our Lord, who is present with us in this meeting.**

*   If your group has partnered with another group, take a moment to report on the experience and to invite creative ideas for continued support.

- Tell the group that you are going to read the story of Jesus praying in the garden of Gethsemane. Invite the participants, as they hear these words, to imagine the intensity of this moment for Jesus as he relinquishes his will to the will of God.

- Read Luke 22:39-44.

- Ask the participants to consider times when they have moved from willfulness to willingness before God. After a minute or two, invite them to share briefly.

- Close with a favorite hymn or "Spirit, Spirit of Gentleness" (TFWS).

SHARING INSIGHTS (45 MINUTES)

Begin by reminding group members of the theme for this week—exploring the meekness of Christ as an alternative stance and sign of God's reign in this world.

1. Let participants review the article and their journal entries for this week. (*5 minutes*)

2. Invite the group members to share their insights. As leader, model the sharing by offering your own brief reflections first. Encourage deep and active listening. (*35 minutes*)

3. Draw out the main points or common themes that emerged from these shared reflections. **What is the Spirit saying to us through these refrains?** (*5 minutes*)

BREAK (10 MINUTES)

DEEPER EXPLORATIONS (45 MINUTES)

Invite the group to explore through lectio divina *the meekness of Christ.*

Introduce the theme. (5 minutes)

The beatitude of meekness invites us to consider a "third way" in this world, a posture that is neither defensive nor aggressive but fully present in love. In situations that aggravate or threaten us, we tend to react with the classic "fight or flight" response. The meekness of Christ shows us a calm and clear faith stance as an alternative. It is what our author calls "the strong gentleness of power under control—the control of God's spirit."

Indicate that we will explore ways to approach, with the meekness of Christ, situations that otherwise try our patience and evoke fearful or harsh reactions. The deep questions behind our explorations are these: **When faced with aggravating, trying, or frightening cir-**

cumstances, how do we stay centered in God's presence with open hands? How can we become a blessing?

We will let the story of Jesus' arrest in Gethsemane help us reflect on the meekness of Christ and our own reactions to violent or provoking situations.

Introduce group lectio *with Luke 22:45-53. (5 minutes)*

Explain that you and the participants will practice a form of group *lectio divina* with this text. Offer a brief explanation of *lectio* if you have group members unfamiliar with the practice (see Leader's Notes, page 60). State that you will read the story three times, inviting focused reflection and journaling after each reading. Those who choose to speak may share briefly when invited. The group is to receive what is shared in quiet receptivity. Explain that after the second reading you will guide their reflections more closely, verse by verse.

Guide the group through the lectio *process. (35 minutes total)*

Let's come now before God with open hands to receive this story and the blessing God is prepared to give each of us through it. As you listen, be aware of Jesus' meek and caring presence throughout this incident and be ready to note in your journal words or phrases that hold your attention.

Read the passage through once slowly. (5 minutes)

- Suggest that participants notice what they hear, sense, or feel as they listen to the story.

- Give them a minute or two of silence after the reading to ponder and journal.

- Then invite those who feel ready to share a single word or phrase that strikes them, while others listen without comment.

Read the passage again a verse or two at a time. (20 minutes)

Invite the participants to visualize the scene and dwell on the images. Say words like these: As I read this story a second time, I invite you to sense points of connection between this story and your life. Make notes in your journal as you feel led.

- Verses 45-46: Pray for an awareness of God's presence and grace at this turning point in the story.

- Verse 47: **Imagine Jesus' feelings when he sees Judas in the crowd.… Feel Jesus' pain as Judas betrays him with a kiss.… What situation in your life conjures up similar feelings of betrayal, suspicion, alienation, or hypocrisy?…**

- Verse 48: **Jesus responds with a question, perhaps to help Judas see what he is doing. What would you have said to Judas?… How do you respond to the adversary, aggressor, or betrayer in your life?…**

- Verses 49-50: **When faced with such a threat, what is your weapon of choice—a physical weapon, biting words, passive aggressive behavior, shunning?…**

- Verse 51: **Listen to Jesus' command: "'No more of this!'" Watch Jesus' response: "He touched [the slave's] ear and healed him."**

- Ask, **From what source did Jesus' meekness in response to might spring? What is the source of your responses? Explore these connections in your journal.** (*3–4 minutes*)

- Welcome a brief sharing of associations and points of connection.

Read the story a third time. (*10 minutes*)

- Ask: **Where is the invitation for you? How is God calling you to a new response? What question or gift do you sense here for living more fully in the blessing of God's kingdom?**

- Give a few minutes for reflection and journaling.

- Invite brief sharing of the sense of God's invitation and challenge to live the way of blessedness.

CLOSING (10 MINUTES)

Revisit Gethsemane. Read aloud again of Jesus' struggle to accept God's will in Luke 22:39-44. Ask the group members to consider God's invitation to them through the story of Jesus' arrest. Encourage them to recall times when they have wrestled with a willingness to be open to God's will.

After a minute of silence, ask the participants if their struggle to move "from willfulness to willingness" bears any relation to the "Closed Hands, Open Hands" meditation from a previous week. If so, have them name the connection they might make.

Rest in the Lord. Gather the group in a circle to practice the last step of *lectio divina* by resting in God's grace. Urge the participants to let all words and thoughts, feelings and struggles give way to simple adoration before God, the fountain of grace and giver of all good gifts.

Sing a quiet song of adoration. After a few minutes of rest, lead them in humming or singing a familiar song of adoration and thanks. Suggestions: "Father, I Adore You"; "Holy, Holy, Holy" (folk version, *The Faith We Sing*).

Pray together. Invite the participants to offer brief prayers as they feel led. Close with the Lord's Prayer.

Say or sing a benediction.

Leader's Note

MEDITATION ON SCRIPTURE (*LECTIO DIVINA*)

We start by reading a Bible passage to take in its content and contours, to hear the words clearly and to observe the characters in action. We go on to reflect on possible meanings and to ponder connections with our lived experience in the world. Then we respond in prayer, sharing our thoughts with God and listening for God to speak to us. Finally, we rest in the word or grace that God gives us, acknowledging what we have received with thanksgiving.

The basic flow can be described in four words:

Read

Reflect

Respond

Rest

The process can and should take many creative forms, depending on the passage and the listener. Yet the basic elements of the process remain fairly constant as trustworthy means of searching beyond the surface of scripture and opening our lives to the searchlight of God's love.

Lectio is a key practice throughout the Companions in Christ series. The daily exercises call us to meditate on scripture in relation to daily life and the themes of this course. The weekly meetings continue this dynamic as we share together the "daily bread" God gives us and practice scriptural meditation and listening prayer in company with one another.

Week 5
A Satisfying Hunger and Thirst

PREPARATION

Prepare yourself spiritually. Pray for an enriched sense of community in your group meeting, and that the reality of God's kingdom might become a deepening hunger for each participant. Read the article for Week 5, reflect on each of the daily exercises, and record responses in your journal.

Prepare materials and the meeting space. Copy "Developing a Rule of Life" (page 65) and "Rule of Life Notes" (page 66) for each group member. Have paper, pencils, and crayons for drawing images, and any current information or ideas about your partner group. Arrange chairs in a circle around a table, and place a candle at its center. Have hymnals or songbooks available, and select songs for the "Opening" and "Closing."

Review the intent of this meeting: to sharpen the desire to live the "good life" for which our souls hunger and thirst.

OPENING (10 MINUTES)

Welcome participants by name.

Set a context.

This week we come to a beatitude central to our understanding of God's kingdom or reign. Hunger and thirst for righteousness are pivotal in our experience of following Jesus.

Join together in worship.

- Light the candle and invite the group to join in praying the "Candle Prayer," or offer your own prayer.

- If your group has a partner group, take a few moments to discuss the partnership.

- Read Matthew 6:33: "**But strive first for the kingdom of God and his righteousness, and all these things will be given to you as well.**" Remind the group that according to some Bible translations Jesus tells his followers "the kingdom of God is within you" (Luke 17:21, NIV and KJV).

- Ralph Waldo Emerson said, "What lies behind us and what lies before us are tiny matters compared to what lies within us." Encourage each person to examine the spirit that resides within.

- Invite silent prayers of thanksgiving for what of God's spirit is within each member of the group and petition for the grace needed to draw each more fully into God's realm.

- Close by singing a song of your choosing. Suggestion: "As the Deer" (TFWS)

SHARING INSIGHTS (45 MINUTES)

Remind the participants of this week's theme—our hunger and thirst for God and the right order of relationships that mark God's realm.

1. Give the participants time to review the article and their journal entries for the week. (*5 minutes*)

2. Ask the participants to share their insights, first from the weekly reading and then from their journal entries. As leader, model the sharing first. Encourage them to practice deep and active listening. (*35 minutes*)

3. Point out common themes you heard during this time, and invite group members to add their perceptions. (*5 minutes*)

BREAK (10 MINUTES)

DEEPER EXPLORATIONS (45 MINUTES)

Guide the group in developing a rule of life for right relationship with God and neighbor.

Introduce the theme. (10 minutes)

Righteousness is God's idea of the good life, a life that is good for everyone and for all creation. We will explore the idea of a "rule of life," a way of life that nourishes our hunger for a deepening relationship with God and that gradually bears fruit in a good life.

Point out that the article, exercises, and our sharing of insights have asked us to become aware of three things:

- the quality of relationship with God for which we hunger and thirst

- the kind of world for which we yearn

- the kind of life we truly desire to live

Two quotes from the article capture especially well some of our hungers. Ask two volunteers from the group to read these quotes from their Participant's Book:

> Those of us with genuine faith and the spark of Christ's hope in our hearts do hunger and thirst for God's right ordering of life. We yearn for an order of life in which people treat others fairly and generously, where no one goes to bed hungry and children do not die from preventable diseases. We thirst for a sense of justice to pervade the choices and actions of all people, especially the powerful. We hunger for the earth to be spared from our own destructiveness, so that its beauty and abundance might be available to our children, grandchildren, and many further generations to come. (Participant's Book, 57)

> Our greatest joy is to allow the life of God's self-giving love to live through us. (Participant's Book, 60)

The questions are these: What leads to such fairness, goodness, and love? What way of life nurtures the relationship with God for which we hunger? What commitments will allow those around us to flourish and our own souls to be deeply satisfied? In other words, how do we get the pattern of Christ's life into us as a regular habit?

At this point the ancient wisdom of a "rule of life" can help. A rule of life is our commitment to a way of living that leads to spiritual growth and transformation—a way of blessedness!

Explain a rule of life as a way of life. (8 minutes)

Hand out the "Developing a Rule of Life" Reflection Sheet and "Rule of Life Notes." Use the "Notes" to expand on the idea of a rule of life. Bring out the key points, then

- Guide the group in looking together at the images suggested under the "Rule of Life Notes." Invite the group to respond to these images or to come up with alternatives.

- Review the examples of personal commitments, and help the group brainstorm some other practices to consider in developing a rule of life.

Begin individual work with the reflection sheet. (12 minutes)

Encourage each person to find a place of solitude to work through the other side of the reflection sheet titled "Developing a Rule of Life."

Engage in the creative process. (10 minutes)

- Distribute paper, pencils, and crayons. Ask participants to

    1. begin outlining a rule of life based on their responses to the Micah passage; OR

    2. draw an image or picture that describes the way of life to which they feel called.

- Emphasize that this process is only a start to developing a rule of life. As we continue our journey through *The Way of Blessedness*, we will come back to the practices we are called to incorporate into our way of life.

Reflect on the process. (5 minutes)

Gather the group and ask people to consider the value of this "Deeper Explorations" process. In what ways was it helpful? What insight or sense of movement have you received? What reservations do you have about developing a rule of life?

CLOSING (10 MINUTES)

Sing a song. Suggestions: "The Servant Song" or "What Does the Lord Require of You" (TFWS)

Read Isaiah 55:1-3. Invite quiet reflection:

- What do we spend our resources on that is not bread for our hunger, drink for our thirst?

- What do we expend our energies on that does not satisfy our souls?

- Hear God's hearty invitation to "eat what is good." What would following this instruction mean in relation to your hunger for what is right, true, just, and beautiful?

Pray in triads. Pray for one another and for the desire and power to do what we intend.

Say a benediction with hands joined.

Developing a Rule of Life

> He has told you, O mortal, what is good; and what does the Lord require of you but to do justice, and to love kindness, and to walk humbly with your God? (Micah 6:8)

Micah gives us a framework for developing a "balanced spiritual diet" for the good life. We could think of "doing justice," "loving kindness," and "walking humbly with God" as three spiritual food groups.

For the purpose of this exercise, we will reverse the order of the three:

"Walk humbly with your God"

What do you most hunger and thirst for in your daily relationship with God?

What regular nourishment of commitments or practices currently feeds this hunger?

What commitments or practices do you need to sustain you, stretch you, and bring greater balance to your relationship with God?

"Love kindness"

What quality of relationship with others (family, friends, strangers) do you hunger and thirst for?

How do you nourish such qualities?

What commitments or practices do you feel you need in order to cultivate greater kindness and mercy in your relationships?

"Do justice"

Where do you most hunger to see God's mending grace at work in this world?

What regular commitments or practices in your life contribute to this mending?

What practices or commitments would help stretch you toward a more just and humane life that avoids harming others and contributes to the healing of human community?

"What does the Lord require of you?"

Develop a balanced diet of commitments and practices that feed your deepest hunger and thirst.

Rule of Life Notes

Key points:
- The Christian spiritual life is a way of life that fosters continual growth in Christ, out of which flows a life lived for the good of others.
- Our relationship with God needs intentional nurturing, just like any other relationship. It requires basic ground rules and boundaries to be healthy.
- Our relationship with God is covenantal. It involves an agreement about how we are to live faithfully as God's people, and how God will relate to us in faithful love. A covenant is a rule of life, a way of being in relationship with God and one another.

Biblical examples of a rule or way of life:
- The Ten Commandments
- Micah 6:8—"What does the Lord require of you…?"
- The Beatitudes

Images of a rule of life:
- A trellis on which a rosebush climbs and spreads to bloom
- A balanced diet that keeps us healthy and energetic to serve

Examples of contemporary Protestant rules of life:
- The "General Rule of Discipleship" used by Covenant Discipleship Groups
- Some church membership vows
- Marriage vows
- The "Piety, Study, and Action" of three-day movements like Cursillo and Emmaus

Examples of personal commitments and practices:
- Half an hour of prayer a day
- Using a breath prayer throughout the day
- Honoring the Sabbath through leisure and recreation
- Devotional reading of the Bible or other spiritual writings
- Meeting regularly with a spiritual friend or small group
- Tithing income for spiritual or charitable purposes
- Working for peace and justice
- Loving attentiveness to family members
- Developing genuine friendships with people of other races/faiths

Week 6

Embracing the Wisdom of Tenderness

PREPARATION

Prepare yourself spiritually. Read the article for Week 6, reflect on the daily exercises, and keep your journal. Practice mercy as much as you are able this week. Pray for the wisdom of tenderness to flower in your group and in your church as a witness to the kingdom of God in this world.

Prepare materials and the meeting space. You will need a copy of the "Jonah Story Reflection Sheet" (page 71) for each participant, newsprint and marker. You will also need to collect pictures cut from newspapers or magazines depicting people in painful or difficult circumstances (persons with AIDS, people living in extreme poverty, war refugees, etc.). You will need one picture for each participant, including you. Arrange the room as usual with a candle at the center of the arrangement. Have hymnals or songbooks available, and select "Opening" and "Closing" songs. Bring to the meeting any current information from or about your partner group.

Review the intent of this meeting: to become more aware of our resistance to mercy and to open our little hearts to God's big heart of mercy for us all.

OPENING (10 MINUTES)

Welcome participants by name.

Set a context.

This week we will explore the rich and challenging practice of mercy. We will identify situations where we resist mercy and will aim to open our hearts to the great reservoir of God's mercy. Our goal is to receive and share God's merciful nature as a witness to God's reign in our lives.

Join together in worship.

- Light the candle and have the group recite together the "Candle Prayer," or offer words like these: **May this flame remind us of the eternal light of God's loving-kindness and boundless mercy.**

- Read the last portion of the Good Samaritan story: **"'Which of these three, do you think, was a neighbor to the man who fell into the hands of the robbers?' He said, 'The one who showed him mercy.' Jesus said to him, 'Go and do likewise'"** (Luke 10:36-37). Remind the group that these words come at the end of this familiar passage. Allow a minute for quiet reflection after you read.

- Read the following quote: **"Flexible and strong, mercy is capable of bearing sorrow's weight and of supporting every honest effort to build new life."**[1]

- Ask the group members to consider silently where they have observed mercy bearing sorrow's weight or supporting an honest effort to build new life.

- Invite sentence prayers from the group.

- Close with a favorite song. Suggestion: "O Lord, Your Tenderness" (TFWS)

SHARING INSIGHTS (45 MINUTES)

Begin by restating the theme for this week—our sharing in the gift of God's mercy.

1. Invite the participants to look back over the article and their journal entries. (*5 minutes*)

2. Ask them to share insights from the weekly reading and journal entries. Offer your own brief reflections first as a model for sharing. Encourage deep and active listening to one another. (*35 minutes*)

3. Invite the participants to identify any common themes they hear that may be clues to God's word for the group. (*5 minutes*)

BREAK (10 MINUTES)

DEEPER EXPLORATIONS (45 MINUTES)

Guide the group in exploring what it means to open our little hearts to God's big heart of mercy.

Introduce the theme. (2 minutes)

Quote the prophet: "I will give them one heart, and put a new spirit within them; I will remove the heart of stone from their flesh and give them a heart of flesh" (Ezek. 11:19).

To be merciful as God is merciful involves a transformation of our hearts from "stone" to "flesh." Only God can accomplish this change in us, but we can actively cooperate by desiring and seeking such transformation.

Suggest that we can begin with the posture we have been practicing: coming before God with open hands, in this case where voices of resentment and retaliation speak loudly in our hearts. The story of Jonah can help us recover this receptive posture.

Set a context for reflection on the story of Jonah. (8 minutes)

- **Jonah doesn't want to go where God wants him to go, because he doesn't want to participate in God's mercy. Jonah's pouting over God's graciousness may help us recognize our own resistance to God's forgiving nature. Yet to see our limited compassion is to see more clearly our great need for God's mercy. Only with divine help can we become more like God.**

- Read the paraphrased story.

- Invite brief responses from the group to this story, particularly about what struck them.

- Now invite people to take their journals and respond to the questions and ideas on the "Jonah Story Reflection Sheet."

Take time for personal journaling with the reflection sheet. (15 minutes)

Allow time for meditation on opening our hearts using images. (10 minutes)

- Set a context: **When we have been hurt or disappointed by others, we, like Jonah, resist extending mercy. How do we move from hearts of stone to hearts of flesh? How can we get God's mercy inside us? Rowan Williams says,**

  Trauma can offer a breathing space,…a door into the suffering of countless other innocents.… In the face of extreme dread, we may become conscious, as people often do, of two very fundamental choices. We can cling harder and harder to the rock of our threatened identity,… or we can let go, and in that letting go, give room to what's there around us—to the sheer impression of the moment, to the need of the person next to you, to the fear that needs to be looked at.… If that happens, the heart has room for many strangers.[2]

Mercy means making room in our hearts for many strangers. Let's practice opening our hearts to those who suffer, even while acknowledging our resistance and limitations.

- Set out news and magazine photos you have collected, facedown on a table.

- Invite each person to select one picture to contemplate.

- Ask each to consider: **What do I see and feel? What invites or repels me? What is the human story behind this picture? How am I moved to pray for this person or these people?** (These questions could be written on newsprint while participants are journaling with the reflection sheet.)

- Suggest that the participants might want to journal briefly with these questions.

Encourage group sharing. (10 minutes)

- Invite the participants to share what they see and the stories they imagine.

- Ask where they felt resistance to opening their hearts to what they saw.

- Ask how they are moved to pray in relation to the picture.

CLOSING (10 MINUTES)

Sing "Ubi Caritas" or "There's a Wideness in God's Mercy."

Continue meditation with picture images. **Imagine again the human stories behind the pictures. What do these people need to forgive?... What might prevent them from extending mercy?... In what ways are you part of this picture?... For what do you need to be forgiven?... Can you imagine the person or people in your picture praying for you?... How does their situation give you perspective on your own struggle to be merciful?...**

Invite spontaneous prayers. End with the Lord's Prayer.

Expand on the beatitude as a benediction:

> **"Blessed are the merciful, for they will receive mercy."**
> **May we share in giving and receiving God's mercy**
> **and so become merciful as God is merciful.**

Jonah Story Reflection Sheet

Get inside Jonah's heart with him as he struggles mightily with God's mercy. Being "in the belly of a whale" for three days is a good metaphor for this struggle.

Think about your life experience. Have you ever thought to yourself, *God, I knew you were going to do this* or *I knew you were like that,* when you felt your own response greatly differed from God's?

When have you felt far from the mercy to which God called you? What kinds of situations tend to bring out this response in you?

Doris Donnelly writes about three common reasons for withholding forgiveness:

1. *You may look weak.* Others may think you have no backbone.
2. *You may be letting someone off the hook.* This person "owes" you and you should be paid back in full. It's a matter of justice.
3. *You may have a responsibility to teach someone a lesson.* This person needs to understand fully what she or he has done and you shouldn't let her or him ever forget it.[3]

For what reasons are you withholding forgiveness from someone now? What makes forgiveness difficult for you?

Paraphrase of the Jonah Story

The word of the Lord came to Jonah saying, "Go to Nineveh, that great city, and preach repentance for their wickedness." But Jonah fled from the presence of the Lord. He found a ship going to Tarshish, paid his fare, and got on board.

But the Lord sent a great storm upon the sea, and the sailors were afraid for their lives. They found Jonah asleep in the hold, and roused him to pray to his god, for he had told them that he was fleeing the presence of the Lord. Then Jonah said, "Pick me up and throw me into the sea and the sea will quiet down. It is because of me that this great storm has come upon you." The men prayed to God not to condemn them for Jonah's life and threw him overboard. Immediately the storm ceased.

Then God sent a great whale to swallow Jonah, and he was in the belly of the whale three days and nights. He prayed a lament of distress and of faith in God's deliverance, and God commanded the fish to spew Jonah out on dry land.

The second time God commanded Jonah to go to Nineveh and preach, he went. He began to walk through the streets, preaching God's judgment, and the people believed him. They repented, putting on sackcloth and ashes. The king himself proclaimed a fast for the whole city and commanded the Ninevites to end their evil ways. So God changed his mind and did not bring calamity upon them.

Then Jonah was furious. He said to God, "Lord, this is exactly why I fled to Tarshish on that ship from the beginning! I knew you were a merciful God, slow to anger and abounding in steadfast love, ready to relent from punishment. So now you can just let me die." The Lord said, "Is it right for you to be angry?" But Jonah went outside the city and sat down to see what would happen to it.

God appointed a plant to come up and provide shade over Jonah's head, and Jonah was happy about the plant. But the next day God sent a worm to attack the plant and it withered, leaving Jonah exposed to the scorching sun and wind. "It is better for me to die than to live," cried Jonah in his frustration.

"Is it right for you to be angry about the plant?" asked God. And Jonah said, "Yes, angry enough to die!" Then the Lord said, "You are concerned about this plant which you did not grow, that came to be in a night and perished in a night. And should I not be concerned about Nineveh, that great city, in which there are more than a hundred and twenty thousand people who don't know their right hand from their left, and also many animals?"

Week 7
Receiving the Vision of God

PREPARATION

Prepare yourself spiritually. Read the article for Week 7, reflect on the daily exercises, and keep your journal. Pray that the Spirit may open your eyes and the eyes of each participant to the fresh joy of God's presence in all of life, including one another.

Prepare materials and the meeting space. Note especially the changes in the time frames for "Sharing Insights" and "Deeper Explorations." Also note as you set up your meeting space that the "Deeper Explorations" process will be a richer experience if no *large* table stands between people in the circle. The best arrangement will be chairs in a circle with a small table for the candle. Make copies of the handout, "Beholding the Blessing in One Another" (page 76). Have your songbooks on hand and choose songs for the "Opening" and "Closing." Bring to the meeting any current information from or about your partner group.

Review the intent of this meeting: to practice seeing God in all things as an expression of purity of heart.

OPENING (10 MINUTES)

Welcome all participants as they enter.

Set a context.

We are moving farther along on our journey through the Beatitudes, experiencing more and more the way of life that makes us citizens of God's realm. This week we will focus on seeing God's gracious presence at the heart of all life, including in one another.

Join together in worship.

- Light the candle and recite the "Candle Prayer," or offer words like these: **May the single flame of this candle remind us of the purity of God's heart that sees all through the eyes of divine love.**

- Read Matthew 16:17: "And Jesus answered him, 'Blessed are you, Simon son of Jonah! For flesh and blood has not revealed this to you, but my Father in heaven.'" Jesus calls Peter blessed, because God has given him eyes to recognize Jesus' true nature. We too are blessed whenever God gives us eyes to see the divine presence in life, especially when we can see it in one another.

- Read this quote from Elisabeth of the Trinity: "**Let us offer ourselves to Him in every moment, in the way that He wants. And when the evening comes, after a dialogue of love which never stopped in our hearts, we will fall asleep in His love.**"

- Encourage the group to rest in these words a little while, imagining what it would be like to spend every minute of one day living as Christ would have us live.

- Ask them to ponder what we might see afresh if we spent a day in this way.

- Close by leading the group in a few verses of "Be Thou My Vision," "Come and See" (TFWS), or a song of your choice.

SHARING INSIGHTS (30 MINUTES)

Begin by reminding group members of the theme for this week—seeing God in all things and seeing as God sees.

1. Ask the participants to review briefly the article for this week and their journal entries for Exercises 1–4 only. Indicate that Exercise 5 will be the basis for the "Deeper Explorations." (*5 minutes*)

2. Invite the participants to share insights from the weekly reading and their journal entries for the first four exercises. Offer your own brief reflections as a model. Encourage deep and active listening. (*20 minutes*)

3. Draw out any common themes that may indicate how the Spirit is moving in the group's midst. (*5 minutes*)

BREAK (10 MINUTES)

DEEPER EXPLORATIONS (60 MINUTES)

Guide the group in the practice of seeing God in people and blessing them with what we see.

Introduce the theme.

We will devote this entire time to the practice of seeing God in one another and blessing each person with a word, phrase, or image for what we see. Through the Beatitudes, Jesus gives us eyes to see what he sees: the blessing of God's reign already emerging in and among us. The Beatitudes can serve as lenses through which we begin to "see God" in our midst.

Provide individual prayer time for beholding the blessing. (15 minutes)

Hand out the prayer aid titled "Beholding the Blessing in One Another," and invite the participants to find a solitary space, inwardly or outwardly, to pray with it.

Share the blessing. (45 minutes)

In light of the time available, establish clear expectations about the approximate number of minutes available for each person to receive and respond to affirmations. Ask everyone to limit their blessings to a few phrases or sentences and to limit their responses similarly.

- Gather the group in a circle of chairs to share the blessings.

- Prayerfully focus the group's attention on one person at a time.

- Moving around the circle, invite other members of the group to bless the person-in-focus with the words or images that express what they behold. After everyone has blessed a person, pause for a prayerful moment to allow the blessing to sink in.

- Give the person-in-focus an opportunity to respond briefly, if he or she wishes (gratitude, question, or confirmation).

- Continue until everyone has received a blessing, including you.

Closing (10 minutes)

Stand and join hands to sing a song of celebration. Suggestions: "Blest Be the Tie That Binds," "Amazing Grace," "Companion Song," or "Open Our Eyes" (TFWS)

Invite prayers of thanksgiving, adoration, and blessing to God.

Say a benediction. Consider using the following words from 1 John 3:2:

> Beloved, we are God's children now;
> what we will be has not yet been revealed.
> What we do know is this: when he is revealed, we will be like him,
> for we will see him as he is.

Beholding the Blessing in One Another
A Prayer Exercise for the Body of Christ Based on the Beatitudes

Beloved, whatever is true, whatever is honorable, whatever is just, whatever is pure, whatever is pleasing, whatever is commendable, if there is any excellence and if there is anything worthy of praise, think about these things. (Phil. 4:8)

Build on what you have already begun in Daily Exercise 5. Review what you entered in your journal for that day. Mark your notes for clarity if this helps you.

Pause in prayer. Allow the eyes of your heart to rest on group members, one at a time. Ask God to open your heart to the sacred mystery of each person before you.

Let the Beatitudes serve as a lens for seeing what Jesus might see. Behold with prayerful openness the ways in which the blessed life of God shines through each of your companions.

Write down in your journal a word, phrase, or image that captures how you see the life of God's reign expressed or emerging in the life of each group member.

Making Peace, An Offering of Love

PREPARATION

Prepare yourself spiritually. Read the article for Week 8, reflect on the daily exercises, and keep your journal. Pray that the Christian vocation to be peacemakers may become a passion in the life of each participant in your group, especially in your own heart.

Prepare materials and the meeting space. "Scenarios for Practicing Peace" (pages 81–82) contains five individual scenes. Make enough copies so that, when cut apart, each member has one scenario. Review the Leader's Note titled "Selecting a Peacemaking Issue" (page 85) and before the meeting select a divisive issue that engages everyone and is generally known. Make one copy apiece of the Reflection Sheet titled "A Path to Becoming Peacemakers" (pages 83–84). Arrange the room with the candle at the center. Have hymnals or songbooks available, and select songs for the "Opening" and "Closing." Bring to the meeting any current information from or about your partner group.

Review the intent of this meeting: to embrace a deep commitment to becoming peaceful persons whose way of life is marked by making peace, a sign that we belong to God's family.

OPENING (10 MINUTES)

Welcome all participants by name as they enter.

Set a context.

Clarence Jordan wrote the following:

> With Jesus, peacemaking involved not merely a change of environment but also a change of heart….God's plan of making peace is not merely to bring about an outward settlement between evil people, but to create people of goodwill.[1]

The whole flow of the Beatitudes leads us to becoming people of goodwill, capable of making peace in all manner of circumstances. This is what we will explore today.

Join together in worship.

- Light the candle as a sign of the peace of Christ in your midst. You may wish to say together the "Candle Prayer."

- Read a brief passage from 2 Corinthians 13:11: **"Finally, brothers and sisters.... Put things in order, listen to my appeal, agree with one another, live in peace; and the God of love and peace will be with you."**

- After a few moments of silence, share these words of Mother Teresa, **"If we have no peace, it is because we have forgotten that we belong to each other."**

- Ask the participants to consider ways we can remember that we belong to one another. Invite them to name what comes to mind.

- Close by leading the group in a song of your choice. Suggestions: "I've Got Peace Like a River" or "Where the Spirit of the Lord Is" (TFWS)

SHARING INSIGHTS (45 MINUTES)

Begin by reminding group members of the theme for this week— that peacemaking is the mark of God's children.

1. Give the participants a few minutes to review the article and their journal entries for this week. (*5 minutes*)

2. Invite the sharing of insights. You may want to offer your own brief reflections first. As always, encourage deep and active listening during this sharing time. (*35 minutes*)

3. Spend a few minutes discussing with the group any common themes you have noticed and listening for the word of God within them. (*5 minutes*)

BREAK (10 MINUTES)

DEEPER EXPLORATIONS (45 MINUTES)

Guide the group in exploring the whole of the Beatitudes as a path to making peace and becoming a peacemaker.

Introduce the theme. (2 minutes)

Remind the group that Week 2 presented the Beatitudes as a progressive whole, "steps into the kingdom, the stairway to spiritual life." Suggest that the Beatitudes can help us see a step-by-step path to peacemaking because they describe how we become persons of peace.

"Peacemakers" is one way to name the calling of Christian disciples. Christians grow not only to see God ("pure in heart"); they grow up to be like God ("peacemakers…children of God"). Indicate that the group is going to practice peacemaking skills and look at issues of peace through the focused lens of all the previous Beatitudes.

Practice peace. (13 minutes)

We're going to begin with a simple and fun exercise to explore our responses as peacemakers to everyday conflicts.

• Distribute the cut-out "Scenarios for Practicing Peace" so everyone has one.

• Ask the group members to take one minute to consider their responses.

• Invite them to read their scenarios and share their responses. Participants who have the same scenario may offer their responses at the same time. Move quickly through all the scenarios.

• Lead a brief conversation on the exercise with a few questions such as:

  1. What do the solutions have in common?

  2. When are conflict situations hardest to solve?

  3. What skills, qualities, or practices seem most critical to peacemaking?

Prepare the path for peace. (30 minutes total for remainder of Deeper Explorations)

(**Reminder:** As leader, you have chosen ahead of time a divisive issue that engages everyone and is generally known.)

Introduce the process. (1 minute)

• **We are going to deal with a real-life peace issue that affects us all.**

• Indicate that the purpose of this exercise is not to resolve a particular issue, much less argue its sides. The purpose is to see how the Beatitudes search us and prepare us inwardly to pursue what makes for peace with God and neighbor.

Present the issue and start the process. (4 minutes)

- Present the peacemaking issue you selected ahead of time that "plagues" you.

- Distribute the reflection sheet entitled "A Path to Becoming Peacemakers."

- Explain the exercise. Point out that we have an opportunity to listen as the Beatitudes call us to the inner conditions of peacemaking.

- Invite participants to revisit the Beatitudes one by one with the aid of the reflection page. Urge them to let the Beatitudes search them, and to respond as honestly as they can about their spiritual progress.

Allow time for individual reflection with worksheet. (15 minutes)

Guide a time of group reflection. (10 minutes)

Ask the group to consider questions like these:

1. What did you find most helpful about this exercise?
2. What did you learn about yourself—your own barriers, willingness, or challenges to grow as a peaceful and peacemaking disciple?

CLOSING (10 MINUTES)

Announce a special preparation for next week. Ask the participants to find or make a symbol of the rule or "way of life" to which they feel called through the Beatitudes. It could be a small, meaningful object to carry with them as a reminder of their commitment to live the way of blessedness. Instruct them to bring the symbol next week for the closing ritual of this journey.

Sing an appropriate song. Suggestion: "Take, O Take Me As I Am" (Iona song)

Invite silent reflection around a final question: **In this last exercise, at what point did you feel God's special address to you?**

Lead a time of prayer, asking the participants to offer a prayer of self-dedication to God based on the way they feel most deeply addressed or convicted. Close with prayer.

Say a benediction: **"Now may the Lord of peace himself give you peace at all times in all ways. The Lord be with all of you"** (2 Thess. 3:16).

Scenarios for Practicing Peace

Imagine yourself as the chief negotiator. In each case, record your peacemaking response.

They: "If she comes, we're not going."
She: "If they come, count me out."
You: _____

_____

_____

She: "Mom, he did it again."
He: "No, I didn't."
She: "Yes, he did."
He: "No, I didn't."
You, the Mom: _____

_____

_____

_____

Country A: "You broke the truce and attacked us!"
Country B: "You provoked us by stealing our supplies!"
You, the Peace Ambassador: _____

_____

_____

_____

They: "We can't have their kind in school."
"Yea, they're so dirty."
"And so noisy."
"They scare me."
You: _____

_____

_____

_____

He: "I'm so sorry, but we have to leave the party."
She: "Do we have to go *now*?"
He: "My office called. They need me."
She: _____

_____

_____

_____

He: "You're late."
She: "No, I'm not."
He: "Yes, you are."
She: "No, I'm not."
He: _____

_____

_____

_____

From *Putting Forgiveness into Practice* by Doris Donnelly (Allen, Tex.: Argus Communications, 1982), 12–13.

A Path to Becoming Peacemakers

REFLECTION SHEET

Describe below the peacemaking issue that plagues you. Then allow the Beatitudes to search you. Listen for their questions to you and for additional questions that may surface. Jot down thoughts about where you are in relation to these questions.

Blessed are the poor in spirit, for theirs is the kingdom of heaven.
You see the problem. Do you see that you are part of it? How far have you come in admitting that you need God's help if you are going to find a way through it? To what extent can you put your own agenda aside long enough to listen—really listen—to God and to others?

Blessed are those who mourn, for they will be comforted.
You see the need, but how deeply concerned are you to do something about it? Do you weep over our distance from God's dream and over the injury that has been inflicted? How will you repent of what has gotten us to this place?

Blessed are the meek, for they will inherit the earth.
Are you now prepared to do meekly whatever God desires? How willing are you to yield entirely to God on this matter, setting aside your attachment to personal agendas and prejudgments? How will you employ your strength under God's direction and gentling Spirit?

Blessed are those who hunger and thirst for righteousness, for they will be filled.
Are you getting by with saying a prayer for those affected, or are you yearning for a lasting peace built on healed relationships and right living? How great is your appetite for hearing and doing the right thing in this situation? To what extent are you willing to go hungry and thirsty, to make sacrifices for the sake of restoring the human family?

Blessed are the merciful, for they will receive mercy.
Are you bent on getting even, or are you willing to forgive what's past for the sake of the mending God wants to do? Are you prepared to give one last chance, or to give as many chances as are needed for wholeness to take root? How far have you walked in the other person's moccasins and seen life from where he or she stands?

Blessed are the pure in heart, for they will see God.
In what ways have you sought the face of God in this matter and allowed the light of God to shine through you? What guile, hypocrisy, or selfishness does God's light expose that makes you less than transparent to the Christ within? How often are you able to see the face of your brother or sister, even perhaps the obscured face of Christ, in those with whom you contend?

Blessed are the peacemakers, for they will be called children of God.
Are you now at peace with God on this matter and at peace with the ways in which this process is transforming you? To what extent have you come to your opponents with open hands and begun the process of rebuilding relationships? Are you trying simply to eliminate conflict, or are you striving for shalom, the well-being and wholeness of God's realm?

Blessed are those who are persecuted for righteousness' sake, for theirs is the kingdom of heaven.
Is your grounding in God firm enough to handle criticism or attack from those who don't want peace and don't like peacemakers? Is your desire to be united with Christ and to share the joy of Christ's life with God greater than your need to avoid pain and conflict? Are you so happy with God's reign that you can suffer the world's unhappiness with *you?*

Leader's Notes

SELECTING A PEACEMAKING ISSUE

For the exercise "Prepare the Path for Peace," select a familiar issue in which everyone can engage. This way, the members can learn from one another's insights and struggles on the inner path to peacemaking. The issue needs to be one that everyone is generally familiar with, has some feelings about, and recognizes as at least potentially divisive. Examples include the national issues of abortion, homosexual rights, or clergy misconduct, or more local issues such as school board debates or points of contention in the church.

Use gentle discipline in helping the group avoid the lure of debate and controversy during the group reflection time. Stay focused on the Beatitudes and the manner in which they challenge us to look beneath the debate to the dispositions of the debaters. The path to peace does not lie "out there" somewhere but in the openness of our hearts and minds to the Spirit of grace and truth. The path does not begin with argument but with listening.

Another option is to allow everyone to choose his or her own issue. The process then becomes more of an individual experience. Participants will still benefit from one another's struggles and insights during the group reflection time, but the process will take longer since each person will need to describe the peacemaking issue.

The Deep Gladness of Suffering Love

PREPARATION

Prepare yourself spiritually. Read the article for Week 9, reflect on the daily exercises, and record thoughts in your journal. Pray that the closure of this small-group experience may be rich with blessing for each participant, and that the Spirit will strengthen the commitments made in this meeting time to ongoing faithfulness in the life of discipleship.

Prepare materials and the meeting space. Remind your members with a postcard, e-mail, or phone call early in the week to bring an object that represents the "way of life" (rule) they take from this small-group journey. Ask them to be prepared to share briefly the significance of their symbol. Make copies of the two handouts "A Covenant Prayer in the Wesleyan Tradition" and the "Closing Litany" for each participant. If your group has partnered with another, you may wish to bring a card or small gift to send that will convey a message of encouragement and blessing and let the partner group know your group is concluding its journey through the Beatitudes. Arrange the room as usual, making space for the symbols to be placed around the candle. Have hymnals or songbooks available, and select songs for the "Opening" and "Closing."

Review the intent of this meeting: to help participants gather the fruit of the Beatitudes by considering their current faith stance and the kingdom "way of life" that enables them to stand firm in ongoing faithfulness.

OPENING (10 MINUTES)

Welcome participants warmly as they enter.

Set a context.

We have come to the final week of our journey through the Beatitudes. Looking back, we can see more clearly the wholeness of the Christian way expressed in the Beatitudes and the integration of all these dispositions of mind and heart. Today we will explore the challenge of the last beatitude, look more closely at the way of life (rule) to which the Beatitudes call us, and affirm one another's commitments as we draw our common journey to a close.

Join together in worship.

- Light the candle in the group's midst, acknowledging Christ's faithful presence with us over these past weeks. Offer words such as these: **As our journey draws to a close, we light this candle once again as a sign of Christ's abiding presence with us. May the flame remind us that Jesus' words continue to illumine the way of blessedness that invites us into the kingdom of God.**

- Read John 13:17, first reminding the group of the setting for this passage:

  It was near the end of Jesus' life on earth as he gathered with his disciples for the Passover feast. During the meal, he rose and began to wash his disciples' feet. These are the words he spoke to them: "If you know these things, you are blessed if you do them."

- Remind the group that Christ is present now, just as he has been through this entire journey. Ask participants to close their eyes and imagine Jesus speaking these words to them personally. (Read the verse again.)

- Invite participants to identify silently one or two discoveries in this journey that particularly stand out. Allow a minute of quiet reflection.

- As leader, share one important way you have benefited from your time with this group; then invite others to offer their thoughts.

- Conclude by leading the group in a prayer or song, such as "Bind Us Together" or "Lord, We Come to Ask Your Blessing" (TFWS).

SHARING INSIGHTS (45 MINUTES)

Remind the group members of the theme for this week—the power of the way of blessedness that helps us stand in the face of trial and difficulty.

1. Give participants a few minutes to review the article and their daily journal entries. (*5 minutes*)

2. Invite shared insights from the weekly reading and their journal entries. As leader, model the sharing by offering your own brief reflections first. Encourage deep and active listening. At an appropriate moment, ask how the members are thinking of this final beatitude in relation to devising a "way of life" that supports living in God's blessing. (*35 minutes*)

3. With the whole group, identify common themes that have emerged. (*5 minutes*)

BREAK (10 MINUTES)

DEEPER EXPLORATIONS (45 MINUTES)

Guide the group in exploring our readiness to inherit fully the life of Christ and to share Christ's sufferings so that we may also share Christ's glory.

Set the context. (10 minutes)

One of the images or metaphors of blessing given to us in the New Testament is "inheritance."

• Give a few examples:

   1. Luke 10:25—"'What must I do to inherit eternal life?'"

   2. Ephesians 1:3, 11—"Blessed…with every spiritual blessing.… In Christ we have also obtained an inheritance."

   3. Romans 8:17—"Heirs of God and joint heirs with Christ…we suffer with him so that we may also be glorified with him."

• Remind the group that the Beatitudes are as complete a picture as Jesus gives us of the blessed life that we, as the children of God, inherit from God and that Jesus came to pass on to us through his life, death, and resurrection.

• Ask: **"How do you feel about receiving this kind of inheritance? Which part of the treasure do you find most challenging?"**

• Give the group a moment to ponder the Beatitudes as a picture of our divine inheritance (ask them to review Matthew 5:3-10 in their Bibles or turn to page 7 in the Participant's Book). Invite brief responses.

Reflect with "A Covenant Prayer in the Wesleyan Tradition." (35 minutes total)

Explain that the group is going to spend some time with a prayer of self-consecration from the Wesleyan tradition. This prayer connects the first and last beatitudes, expressing the complete open-handedness the group has been practicing all along their journey. It invites and challenges them to receive joyfully the full inheritance with which they have been blessed in Christ.

Distribute the handout titled "A Covenant Prayer in the Wesleyan Tradition" with its questions for reflection.

- Allow solitary time for meditation on the prayer and response to the questions. (*15 minutes*)

- Have the group listen in pairs. (*10 minutes*)

  1. Ask everyone to pair up. Each person will have five minutes to talk about responses to the Covenant Prayer and about practices that make up a part of his or her "way of life" (rule) as a follower of Christ.

  2. The aim of the listener is to hear and ask clarifying questions. Listeners limit their speech to prayerful and respectful questions; they make no statements and provide no counsel.

- Gather the whole group for brief reflection on the value of this exercise. (*10 minutes*) Keep these questions in mind as the group reflects together:

  1. Do the participants have a clear sense of areas where they have grown in this journey through the Beatitudes?

  2. What "way of life" (rule) is emerging from this experience?

CLOSING (10 MINUTES)

Begin by asking the group to read aloud the Covenant Prayer.

Sing a song of your choosing, or "Bring Forth the Kingdom" (TFWS).

Join in the ritual of shared symbols.

- Remind the group members that you asked them to bring a symbol representing the "way of life" (rule) that they will carry with them from this journey through the Beatitudes. Invite them now (1) to share the significance of this symbol and (2) to describe the kind of support they would like to ask the group for as they commit to the way of life their symbol represents.

- Ask each participant to share his or her symbol, speaking briefly to the two points above.

- After sharing, have each person place his or her symbol on the table so that the symbols surround the Christ candle. Invite the group to observe these symbols in a spirit of thanks and hope.

- Offer a brief prayer of consecration:

  God of all blessing,
  In hope and trust we offer ourselves to you,
      along with these symbols of the way of life you call us to.
  Help us to be faithful witnesses
      to the beauty, wonder, and transforming power of your reign.
  In the blessed name of Christ we pray. Amen.

- Return each symbol to the appropriate person. Say words such as these to the group: **We leave this place, taking with us these symbols to remind us of the way of life to which we commit ourselves as citizens of the kingdom of God.**

- Lead the group in the "Closing Litany" (pages 93–94).

Sing a closing song (optional). Suggestion: "Lord, Be Glorified" (TFWS)

A Covenant Prayer in the Wesleyan Tradition

I am no longer my own, but thine.

Put me to what thou wilt, rank me with whom thou wilt.

Put me to doing, put me to suffering.

Let me be employed by thee or laid aside for thee,

    exalted for thee or brought low by thee.

Let me be full, let me be empty.

Let me have all things, let me have nothing.

I freely and heartily yield all things

    to thy pleasure and disposal.

And now, O glorious and blessed God,

    Father, Son, and Holy Spirit,

    thou art mine, and I am thine. So be it.

And the covenant which I have made on earth,

    let it be ratified in heaven. Amen.

Questions for Reflection

1. What do you find in this prayer that you are ready to say yes to? What gives you pause? How would you paraphrase this prayer to take its meaning for yourself?

2. What do you feel God is calling you to be and do through the Beatitudes?

3. What elements of a "way of life" (regular pattern of spiritual practices) do you need in order to sustain your availability to God and your continued communion with Christ? How do you plan to incorporate these practices into your life?

Closing Litany

Leader: Jesus said, "Blessed are the poor in spirit, for theirs is the kingdom of heaven."
O God, help us to know the happiness of relying on your grace in all things.
Group: Thank you for the example of Jesus, who though he was rich became poor for our sake. By his weakness we are made strong. Blessed are the poor in spirit, for theirs is the kingdom of heaven.

Leader: Jesus said, "Blessed are those who mourn, for they will be comforted."
O God, we are fearful of death and discouraged by evil. Unless you speak to us we will be overcome by grief.
Group: Thank you for Jesus Christ who overcame sin and death in every form. Abiding in him we find hope and comfort. Blessed are those who mourn, for they will be comforted.

Leader: Jesus said, "Blessed are the meek, for they will inherit the earth."
O God, restrain our anxious or arrogant reactions and teach us true gentleness. Show us how to give you our full strength and how to cherish this magnificent earth.
Group: Thank you for Jesus our teacher, who called us friends. In friendship with him may we find companionship with all people and all creatures. Blessed are the meek, for they will inherit the earth.

Leader: Jesus said, "Blessed are those who hunger and thirst for righteousness, for they will be filled."
O God, give us a deep hunger for you and a strong thirst for your right ways in this world.
Group: Thank you for Jesus who lived your right ways with perfect love. By his spirit give us freedom to live in justice and mercy. Blessed are those who hunger and thirst for righteousness, for they will be filled.

Leader: Jesus said, "Blessed are the merciful, for they will receive mercy."
O God, you alone have a heart of true mercy. Without your help we become trapped in harsh judgment and resentment, blinded to our own need for your mercy.
Group: Thank you for Jesus who showed us your mercy, forgiving the worst we could do. Receiving his mercy, may we freely share it. Blessed are the merciful, for they will receive mercy.

Leader: Jesus said, "Blessed are the pure in heart, for they will see God."
O God, to see you is indescribable joy. Yet we live with double vision and divided hearts.
Group: Thank you for Jesus whose words and deeds were undivided. As we live in communion with him may our vision be clarified until we see you in all. Blessed are the pure in heart, for they will see God.

Leader: Jesus said, "Blessed are the peacemakers, for they will be called children of God."
O God, how little we have shown ourselves to be your children, sowing suspicion and discord, division and strife through this world and even in your church. Show us, we pray, the way to peace.
Group: Thank you for Jesus Christ, who has broken down our walls of division, reconciling us to you and to one another in love. In his strength may we live in peace and sow peace. Blessed are the peacemakers, for they will be called children of God.

Leader: Jesus said, "Blessed are those who are persecuted for righteousness' sake, for theirs is the kingdom of heaven."
O God, we are too often afraid to risk ourselves for your truth. Give us firmness of faith and courage to obey your way of life in every circumstance.
Group: Thank you for Jesus Christ, who suffered persecution and abuse to give us fullness of life. May we fearlessly follow him and confess his light before the world. Then we may know the happiness of belonging to your reign in this world and the next. Blessed are those who are persecuted for righteousness' sake, for theirs is the kingdom of heaven.

Leader: Now may the risen Lord Jesus Christ bless you and keep you; the Lord make his face to shine upon you, and be gracious to you; the Lord lift up the light of his countenance upon you, and give you peace. Amen.

Notes

PREPARATORY MEETING

1. Eugene H. Peterson, *Working the Angles: The Shape of Pastoral Integrity* (Grand Rapids, Mich.: William B. Eerdmans, 1987), 103–4.

WEEK 1: EXPLORING THE BLESSED LIFE

1. Lloyd John Ogilvie, *Lord of the Impossible* (Nashville, Tenn.: Abingdon Press, 1984), 28.

WEEK 2: EMBRACING OUR SPIRITUAL POVERTY

1. Henri J. M. Nouwen, *With Open Hands* (Notre Dame, Ind.: Ave Maria Press, 1972), 154.

WEEK 3: TEARS AS ANGUISH, TEARS AS GIFT

1. Adapted from *Way to Live: Christian Practice for Teens* (Nashville, Tenn.: Upper Room Books, 2002), 251–59.
2. Ibid, 253.

WEEK 6: EMBRACING THE WISDOM OF TENDERNESS

1. John S. Mogabgab, "Editor's Introduction," *Weavings: A Journal of the Christian Spiritual Life* 15, no. 5 (September/October 2000): 2.
2. Rowan Williams, *Writing in the Dust* (Grand Rapids, Mich.: William B. Eerdmans, 2002), 59–60.
3. Doris Donnelly, *Putting Forgiveness into Practice* (Allen, Tex.: Argus Communications, 1982), 46.

WEEK 8: MAKING PEACE, AN OFFERING OF LOVE

1. Clarence Jordan, *Sermon on the Mount* (Valley Forge, Pa.: Judson Press, 1993), 20.

Evaluation

When your group has completed the *Companions in Christ: The Way of Blessedness* resource, please share your insights and experiences in relation to the questions below. Use additional paper if needed.

1. Describe your group's experience with *Companions in Christ: The Way of Blessedness*.

2. Did the resource lead your participants to live more fully within the reign of God in any new and concrete ways? If it did, please share your experience with us in this evaluation or through the discussion room at www.companionsinchrist.org.

3. How could *Companions in Christ: The Way of Blessedness* be improved?

4. Do you have follow-up plans for your group? What resource do you plan to use, or what kinds of resources are you looking for?

Mail to: *Companions in Christ*
           Upper Room Ministries
           P. O. Box 340012
           Nashville, TN 37203-0012   or fax: 615-340-7178